Are You
CHAIRING A BOARD
by the Seat of Your Pants?

by
Susan M. Scribner
SCRIBNER & ASSOCIATES
49 Coronado Avenue
Long Beach, California 90803
(562) 433-6082 (voice or TDD)
(562) 439-3025 (Fax)
INTERNET: scribner@aol.com.

© 1997, Scribner & Associates. All Rights Reserved.
Copy this and you'll be in the Hot Seat. See you in court. Have a nice day.

THE NONPROFIT IN YOUR FACE TRILOGY!

by Susan M. Scribner

HOW TO ASK FOR MONEY WITHOUT FAINTING!

Are You CHAIRING A BOARD by the Seat of Your Pants?

Scribner & Associate publications are available in a variety of languages. Discounts are provided for multiple orders. Please refer to the order form at the end of this publication to contact Scribner & Associates.

...AND FOR YOU COMPUTER GEEKS:

Scribner's In Your Face training electronic books are available from
Capitol Publications
(800) 392-7886

(include nasty interactive tests and great search systems!)

The information contained in this and all Scribner & Associate publications represents the opinions of the author. Nothing contained herein is to be considered as the rendering of legal advice. Readers are encouraged to obtain advice from their own counsel. Honest. All forms, sample agreements and suggestions enclosed in the publications are intended for informational and educational purposes only.

CONGRATULATIONS

Welcome to the world of the unknown!

I became a Board Chair because I missed a meeting ...so one of the first things I learned was to SHOW UP!

I don't know about you, but I did not attend Board Chair College. I wanted to be an effective Chair or President but I didn't know how. I soon found out that I wasn't alone!

The fact of the matter is that there is NO BOARD COLLEGE. We have been passing bad Board information around like fruitcakes during the holidays (no offense to those of you who like fruitcakes). Generations of lousy Board Chairs have been created and many serve on multiple Boards. Why? I guess we assume a Board Fairy visits the Chairs after elections and sprinkles wisdom and knowledge on their heads about How to Run a Meeting, the Roles of Board and Staff, How to Read a Financial Statement and Delegation Techniques...

Anyone who agrees to Chair a Board, committee or any type of group deserves tremendous regard and respect! It isn't easy and it is rarely fun. It is my hope that this guidebook will help you lighten up a little, share your responsibilities more, be the most effective leader that you can, maintain a life of your own and, believe it or not, have fun!

By the way, thank you! We need you!

Sincerely,

Susan M. Scribner

WHAT TO DO WITH THIS GUIDEBOOK!

CHAIRING A BOARD is designed to help you develop leadership skills that are comfortable for you and helpful to your Board (although many of the issues apply to any type of group). But first you have to identify the problems, and some of them may be **yours**!

•Review the various types of Chairs in the first section of the guidebook. Find yourself! Specific solutions are checked along the side of each page. You'll notice that many problems require the same solutions, and most of them are easy.

•The last section of the guidebook contains further information about the recommended solutions. Good Luck!

1   © 1997, Scribner & Associates

IT HAD TO BE YOUUUU...

Okay, it is time to bite the bullet... There are many types of Chairs or Presidents. One of the first steps in Chair Recovery is to identify those nasty little traits or habits that we each have - and then try to improve them or leave them alone!

CHAIRING A BOARD includes a number of types of leadership styles... review them as honestly as you can, and try to identify traits that may apply to you. Talk to other members of your Board or group about them. You'll be surprised how supportive (and deadly honest) everyone can be.

Like any good "decor," each Board, committee or group must have its own special style. Its Chair must be functional and easily accessible. A good chair has qualities that fit the rest of the room; it is consistent. However, sometimes our styles become a bit "uncomfortable":

SWIVEL CHAIRS (swing one way then another)

STRAIGHT BACK CHAIRS (very rigid)

LOUNGE CHAIRS (rarely do anything)

BEACH CHAIRS (head in the sand)

FOLDING CHAIRS (give in easily)

DIRECTOR'S CHAIRS (control freaks)

ELECTRIC CHAIRS (always on the hot seat)

HIGH CHAIRS (gripe all the time - known to throw food on occasion)

STACKING CHAIRS (appoint a lot of other leaders)

COUCHES (co-chairs - the best way for no one to do anything)

BEAN BAG CHAIRS (mold easily and give in to group pressure)

LOVE SEATS (endearing people who no one wants to confront)

VIRTUAL CHAIRS (   )

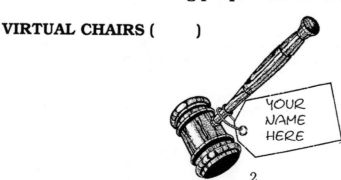

© 1997, Scribner & Associates

HELP HELP HELP

Are You Chairing A Board by the Seat of Your Pants?

Table of Contents

Types of Chairs   Page

Swivel Chairs	4
Straight Back Chairs	5
Lounge Chairs	6
Beach Chairs	7
Folding Chairs	8
Director's Chairs	9
Electric Chairs	10
High Chairs	11
Stacking Chairs	12
Couches	13
Bean Bag Chairs	14
Love Seats	15
Virtual Chairs	16

What's in a Name	17
What's My Job (By-Laws vs. My-Laws)	21
Understanding By-Laws (Wow! A New Concept!)	24
Parliamentary Procedures (Non-deadly Meetings)	41
Bob's Rules of Disorder	46
Sixty Second Minutes	49
Mini Committee Reports	50
Meeting Mandates	51
Lonely at the Top (Getting Others to Help)	52
The Business of the Board	57
Smile When You Say That (Staff/Volunteer Partners)	62
What to Include in a Chair Kit	65
About the Chair of this Guidebook	
Order in the Court (Uh-oh, there are more publications)	

© 1997, Scribner & Associates

SWIVEL CHAIRS

SOUND FAMILIAR?

- Make a decision (or so it appears) and then "swing back" in the opposite direction
- Can be totally unpredictable; one never knows which way they will go
- Often influenced by the strongest members of the group, rather than their own convictions
- Prefer to leave major issues to Executive Committees or other groups without having to take personal responsibility

UH OH

Swivel Chairs are great at driving both members and staff crazy as they most often cannot be counted on to back up a decision or support tough actions.

These Chairs have been known to change mission statements to keep an agency solvent and recruit people they don't know to join the group so it appears that the agency is "doing the right thing."

Often disguised as endearing people, many Swivel Chairs are very kind and want to please everyone. That's part of their problem. After a while, volunteers and staff find that this is not a person who can be relied upon consistently. Good members start to leave and less than well meaning members tend to push the rest of the members around. Executive Committees love to bully Swivel Chairs and usually succeed.

HELP!

Swivel Chairs need support and help. It is not that these leaders are "wishy washy;" it's that they often aren't sure what the group expects of them. Many are afraid to appear to be "too controlling" - so in an effort to be fair to everyone, the group is basically left without a leader at all. The best way to help Swivel Chairs is to give them permission to do their job... help them learn and support them.

So Now What?
Throw in the Towel

🪑 Hold a Special Meeting

Get Outside Expertise

🪑 Clarify Expectations

Celebrate!

Thank Your Board

Clarify Board Roles

Analyze and Recruit

Change Meeting Style

Clarify Terms of Office

Leave Town

Clarify Goals, Objectives

Check Your By-Laws

🪑 Just Say No

🪑 Just Say Yes

© 1997, Scribner & Associates

STRAIGHT BACK CHAIRS

SOUND FAMILIAR?

- Often very rigid and controlling leaders
- Known to remove items from agendas to keep them from the Board or group
- Tend to use rules as a means to control rather than guide
- Maintain a small circle of "insiders"
- Often make decisions without consulting other members of the Board or staff

UH OH

Straight Back Chairs are tough to work with. They are often very bright people with great intentions. They want to move things along quickly... they want to minimize what they consider to be "unnecessary" discussions about issues.

Most of these Chairs are well motivated, but unfortunately end up robbing Board or group members of the most important element in organizational development... ownership. Members of the group often feel like "witnesses" rather than participants; many are afraid to speak out or feel reluctant to challenge a decision that has been made without their input.

HELP!

Unless you want the Board to diminish to one, action steps need to be taken with these Chairs. Communication and role clarification is imperative. The discussion does not need to be combative, but it needs to be honest. Board or group members and staff have an obligation to lend their skills to the agency as well. In order to do so, they must truly be involved in the process.

So Now What?

Throw in the Towel

🪑 Hold a Special Meeting

Get Outside Expertise

🪑 Clarify Expectations

Celebrate!

Thank Your Board

🪑 Clarify Board Roles

Analyze and Recruit

🪑 Change Meeting Style

Clarify Terms of Office

Leave Town

Clarify Goals, Objectives

Check Your By-Laws

Just Say No

Just Say Yes

5

© 1997, Scribner & Associates

LOUNGE CHAIRS

SOUND FAMILIAR?

- Yawn
- Show up for meetings, but rarely do much beyond that
- Often known to be very active - for other groups or organizations
- Great in emergencies but difficult with consistent, day to day responsibilities
- Terrific at Phone Tag
- Often see the agenda for the first time upon arrival at the meeting
- Anxious to end meetings on time so they can go to another one and do nothing there as well

UH OH

Lounge Chairs are interesting people. Often they are extremely committed to the agency or the cause, but it doesn't appear that an adequate amount of their time or resources are devoted to the work of the group.

Most often these Chairs know what their role is supposed to be but, unless there is a crisis, they tend to let things move along on their own. Sometimes that's just fine, but this type of "non-leadership" is not very inspirational for the rest of the Board or group.

Lounge Chairs also are breeding grounds for inappropriate staff control. Without clear and consistent guidance from a volunteer leader, staff is literally forced to run the agency and then, later, chastised for doing so.

HELP!

Lounge Chairs used to be great when we didn't need as much Board or group involvement. Times have changed and strong leadership is more important than ever before.

These Chairs often will rise to the occasion if they are challenged to do so and if expectations are clarified. Occasionally, it is time for them to move to another position that doesn't require as much responsibility yet maintain a positive and active role within the organization. It might help to bring in an outside party to deal with this important issue.

So Now What?

Throw in the Towel
Hold a Special Meeting
Get Outside Expertise
Clarify Expectations
Celebrate!
Thank Your Board
Clarify Board Roles
Analyze and Recruit
Change Meeting Style
Clarify Terms of Office
Leave Town
Clarify Goals, Objectives
Check Your By-Laws
Just Say No
Just Say Yes

© 1997, Scribner & Associates

BEACH CHAIRS

SOUND FAMILIAR?

- Whoops, did we have a meeting scheduled?
- Known for forgetting assignments, especially their own
- Often lose minutes or forget they were necessary in the first place
- Sometimes aren't sure about where the records of the agency are located
- Almost always make the agency look good to outsiders
- Usually conduct very enjoyable meetings

UH OH

Beach Chairs are kind of cute. Sometimes they just aren't with the program, but they usually mean well. They tend to forget what they were supposed to do between meetings and cram all their efforts into the afternoon before - or right before the meeting starts.

These Chairs most often accept the position because no one else was willing to and they often are exceptionally busy people to start with. Other Board or group members tend to coast along with Beach Chairs, as they don't really want to accept more responsibility either.

Beach Chairs are common with nonprofit organizations or groups which do not have staff. Things disappear or tasks just don't get accomplished sometimes. These groups, however, tend to include people who enjoy being with each other and find the mission of the organization secondary to the experience. This is okay - if you are a bowling league...

HELP!

Most nonprofit organizations were formed for very important reasons. In order to meet the needs of our clients most effectively, we all have to take our jobs seriously. Board contracts and clarification of roles and responsibilities are becoming more popular on the part of volunteers who want the best use made of their time. Board Chairs have an obligation to get their act together and treat the agency like a business.

So Now What?

Throw in the Towel

Hold a Special Meeting

Get Outside Expertise

🪑 Clarify Expectations

Celebrate!

Thank Your Board

🪑 Clarify Board Roles

Analyze and Recruit

Change Meeting Style

Clarify Terms of Office

Leave Town

🪑 Clarify Goals, Objectives

Check Your By-Laws

Just Say No

Just Say Yes

© 1997, Scribner & Associates

FOLDING CHAIRS

SOUND FAMILIAR?

"We can't, we can't"
"I don't think we should change the way we've been doing this"
"Sure, if that is what you all want to do"
"I don't care one way or the other"
"Maybe if we just wait and see what happens"

UH OH

Sigh. Folding Chairs cave in to staff, volunteers and other members of the Board or group. They often have opinions of their own, but don't trust their own judgement enough to challenge the members.

Most Folding Chairs are reluctant to try new things or "make waves." They often are not involved with the agency beyond attending meetings so their emotional connections with the clients or the mission in general tend to be minimal.

Some of these Chairs have long tenures of leadership with their agencies. This lack of rotation of leadership tends to keep nonprofits from moving forward or trying new ideas.

HELP!

Change is hard at all levels. One of the reasons that nonprofits have Boards and diverse leadership is to challenge ideas; try new ways of doing things; and remain flexible to client, volunteer and donor needs. Strong leadership provides an atmosphere of flexibility, new ideas and challenges. Caving in each time a unique opportunity arises is definitely not in the best interest of the clients nor the agency's support staff and volunteers.

So Now What?

Throw in the Towel

Hold a Special Meeting

Get Outside Expertise

🪑 Clarify Expectations

Celebrate!

Thank Your Board

🪑 Clarify Board Roles

Analyze and Recruit

Change Meeting Style

🪑 Clarify Terms of Office

Leave Town

Clarify Goals, Objectives

Check Your By-Laws

Just Say No

🪑 Just Say Yes

© 1997, Scribner & Associates

DIRECTOR'S CHAIRS

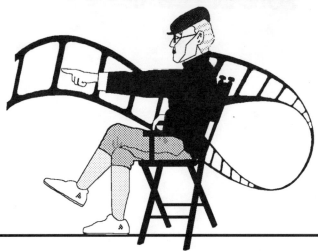

SOUND FAMILIAR?

- Rigid, rigid, rigid
- Rules, rules, rules
- Great ceremonies, but few opportunities for real discussions
- Always make sure that appearances are proper and agency image is positive
- Permit very little input from members of the Board or staff
- Reluctant to seek help so that weaknesses will not be exposed

UH OH

Bullies. Often these types of Chairs are tough to deal with and it is astounding how often they get reelected. Maybe other members are afraid that they will pick up the same, nasty disease if they hold the gavel.

Strangely enough, Director Chairs often keep agencies running quite smoothly - that is, until they or the entire Board and staff leave. Then things tend to fall apart rather quickly.

Director Chairs do not delegate meaningful tasks to either staff or other members of the Board, discouraging the use of both inside and outside expertise. This type of control can lead to real legal and ethical problems for an organization if one keeps in mind that ALL members of the Board are equally responsible, regardless of their roles.

HELP!

It is often useless to expect a Director Chair to lighten up. It is not possible for members of the Board to change anyone's DNA.

Often, several Board members will conduct an endless number of "secret meetings," taking valuable time away from the business of the agency. A lot of plotting and planning, but often little action. This is a serious issue which needs to be prevented from the beginning and confronted the moment it is discovered.

So Now What?

Throw in the Towel
- Hold a Special Meeting

Get Outside Expertise
- Clarify Expectations

Celebrate!

Thank Your Board
- Clarify Board Roles

Analyze and Recruit
- Change Meeting Style
- Clarify Terms of Office

Leave Town

Clarify Goals, Objectives
- Check Your By-Laws
- Just Say No

Just Say Yes

© 1997, Scribner & Associates

ELECTRIC CHAIRS

SOUND FAMILIAR?

- Make many plans without the Board's or staff's knowledge then "announce them" at the meetings
- Take actions for the "good of the agency" when in public without regard to Board policies
- Move meetings or conduct them at their own convenience

UH OH

Such a shock these Chairs give!

They often are full of surprises but, unfortunately, many of them are not in the best interest of the agency! Electric Chairs almost always mean well. They want to make things easier for everybody but don't often consider the consequences of their actions.

These Chairs are very quick to create solutions - even when there are not any problems to solve. They are action focused and tend to live by the rules of "fire, ready, aim."

Electric Chairs often have a tight hold on an agency. Their energy is appreciated and other members are not inclined to want to "take the job" because it appears too time consuming and overwhelming. It appears as such because the Chairs make it look that way...

HELP!

It doesn't have to be so hard to be a decent Chair of a Board or group. A good Chair investigates, delegates and shares the responsibility of leadership. No surprises. Electric Chairs keep a very high tension in an agency when this valuable energy should be focused on the clients instead. They need to be educated, calmed and focused.

So Now What?

Throw in the Towel

🪑 Hold a Special Meeting

Get Outside Expertise

🪑 Clarify Expectations

Celebrate!

Thank Your Board

🪑 Clarify Board Roles

Analyze and Recruit

🪑 Change Meeting Style

Clarify Terms of Office

Leave Town

🪑 Clarify Goals, Objectives

Check Your By-Laws

Just Say No

Just Say Yes

© 1997, Scribner & Associates

HIGH CHAIRS

SOUND FAMILIAR?

- **My way or the highway**
- **Known to throw food at meetings on occasion**
- **Often stubborn and unwilling to discuss an issue**
- **Discourage group input**
- **Possess the ability to individually embarrass members of the group**

UH OH

High Chairs are brats.

Often they are loud, immature and not inclined to take any advice especially from a member of the Board or staff. They tend to be resistant to change and, like many toddlers, are stubborn and demanding.

These Chairs often will push an agency to its limit and then some. Occasionally they can be risk takers beyond reason... if only to make a point.

High Chairs tend to be very smart. Don't be fooled by their actions. Obviously, temper tantrums worked for them when they were younger so the habit remains.

HELP!

Stop it. High Chairs need to be confronted. Rules need to be clarified and both Board and staff members have to take action in the best interest of the agency.

High Chairs tend to back down when confronted. They often truly want to be liked and respected but just don't know how to do their jobs so they do what comes naturally...act out.

So Now What?

Throw in the Towel

Hold a Special Meeting

Get Outside Expertise

🪑 **Clarify Expectations**

Celebrate!

Thank Your Board

🪑 **Clarify Board Roles**

Analyze and Recruit

🪑 **Change Meeting Style**

Clarify Terms of Office

Leave Town

Clarify Goals, Objectives

Check Your By-Laws

🪑 **Just Say No**

Just Say Yes

© 1997, Scribner & Associates

STACKING CHAIRS

SOUND FAMILIAR?

- LOVE to assign work (and responsibility) to others without taking any themselves
- Create very large structures...large and ineffective
- Known to invite people to work on special projects and even appoint them to the Board without telling anyone
- Keep things very confusing

UH OH

Stacking Chairs aren't responsible. Even though they are, they aren't. Ask them. "I appointed so and so to do that job, it's not my fault," or "that's what we hired the staff to do."

Stacking Chairs are slippery. They appear to be in charge and fair when in fact they often delegate without instruction and clarification. This keeps them in control and keeps the crowd confused. They increase the organization's structure like wire coat hangers that clone themselves in the middle of the night in closets.

Management by overload is the theme for Stacking Chairs. One will often find many useless committees on these Boards. Except the Executive Committee. That one tends to work well with Stacking Chairs. After all, it is the smallest group that they can control to control everything else.

HELP!

Stacking Chairs can take nonprofits to the breaking point, since few people have the energy to confront them. More often than not, Stacking Chairs are just not sure about their role. They include *more* people and expand the structure to protect themselves and not expose their problems. Most Stacking Chairs mean well - but bigger isn't always better...

So Now What?

Throw in the Towel

Hold a Special Meeting

Get Outside Expertise

Clarify Expectations

Celebrate!

Thank Your Board

Clarify Board Roles

Analyze and Recruit

Change Meeting Style

Clarify Terms of Office

Leave Town

Clarify Goals, Objectives

Check Your By-Laws

Just Say No

Just Say Yes

© 1997, Scribner & Associates

COUCHES

SOUND FAMILIAR?

- Co-Chairs - a great way to have no one in charge
- I thought HE did it, I thought SHE did it
- Often create co-chairs for their committees
- Create a great deal of confusion among staff and other Board or group members
- Believed to be Politically Correct (not)
- Tend to be close friends or close enemies...either way, too close for comfort

UH OH

Couches or Co-chairs are a pain in the neck. Even to each other.

Often created to "make things easier," and "share responsibility," Co-chairs usually end up creating confusion, as it is impossible to tell Who's On First.

Co-chairs usually are talented, committed men and women. But neither is committed enough to do the job. They tend to be exceptionally busy and hope, through this partnership, that work can be divided evenly and fairly. Unfortunately - more often than not the opposite occurs - staff and volunteers don't know where the buck stops. It has to stop somewhere.

HELP!

The role of the Chair of the Board has to be made more humane for all involved. Positions need to be clarified, focused and responsibilities delegated to strong agency committees. If the agency needs help or is overloading its leadership, then it may very well be time to expand the organization rather than split the positions.

So Now What?

Throw in the Towel

Hold a Special Meeting

🪑 Get Outside Expertise

Clarify Expectations

Celebrate!

Thank Your Board

🪑 Clarify Board Roles

Analyze and Recruit

Change Meeting Style

Clarify Terms of Office

Leave Town

🪑 Clarify Goals, Objectives

Check Your By-Laws

🪑 Just Say No

Just Say Yes

© 1997, Scribner & Associates

BEAN BAG CHAIRS

SOUND FAMILIAR?

- **Easily molded**
- **Anxious to please everybody**
- **Rarely inclined to take a strong stand on behalf of clients**
- **Intent on "being fair" to everybody**
- **Not inclined to hold members accountable for their actions**

UH OH

Sweet people. Inclined to start collectives if they are not monitored appropriately.

Most Bean Bag Chairs just do not understand what is expected of them from the members of the group. Often they don't have strong leadership skills and do not want to be overbearing. Unfortunately, they end up being figure heads instead of leaders...

Bean Bag Chairs make it difficult for staff and group or Board members to take action. They aren't sure if they will be backed up and have little sense of security.

The groups or Boards often are left without a leader at all.

HELP!

Bean Bag Chairs need training. They need to "get with the program" and realize that groups and Boards need strong leadership they can respect, rely on and follow. This does not mean that groups want dictators, but guidance and leadership by example are invaluable tools in any group.

So Now What?

Throw in the Towel

Hold a Special Meeting

Get Outside Expertise

Clarify Expectations

Celebrate!

Thank Your Board

Clarify Board Roles

Analyze and Recruit

Change Meeting Style

Clarify Terms of Office

Leave Town

Clarify Goals, Objectives

Check Your By-Laws

Just Say No

Just Say Yes

© 1997, Scribner & Associates

LOVE SEATS

SOUND FAMILIAR?

- **Extensive history with organization**
- **Very clear opinions about the agency's programs and future**
- **Extremely energetic and giving to the organization**
- **Locked into a set of old emotional baggage or rules... "this won't work, it didn't before, etc."**
- **Reluctant to accept change**

UH OH

Love Seats are to be cherished members of the Board or group. They often are founders or were part of the driving force that created our organizations in the first place.

Love Seats' motives and compassion usually are unquestionable. Unfortunately, the world has changed since the agency started and they have not kept up. Love Seats often are disappointed because other members of the Board or group are not working as hard as they are... not understanding that things have changed; many people have multiple jobs and many commitments in their lives.

Nobody likes to confront a Love Seat. After all, look at the time they have put in, the work they have done... it isn't easy to change - but each member of the group has a responsibility to do what is best for the clients, not the survival of the agency or its founders.

HELP!

Love Seats should not be put down. Rather, they should be elevated, celebrated and acknowledged. They should serve a role in the agency that is of importance and relied upon. Most often they should not remain as Chairs but can be more effective as members of endowment councils and other important support groups.

So Now What?

Throw in the Towel

Hold a Special Meeting

Get Outside Expertise

Clarify Expectations

Celebrate!

Thank Your Board

Clarify Board Roles

Analyze and Recruit

Change Meeting Style

Clarify Terms of Office

Leave Town

Clarify Goals, Objectives

Check Your By-Laws

Just Say No

Just Say Yes

© 1997, Scribner & Associates

VIRTUAL CHAIRS

SOUND FAMILIAR?

•**Something is missing from this picture...namely, a Chair!**

UH OH

Great. All dressed up and no where to go.

Virtual Chairs usually are elected when they miss a meeting or agree to serve because no one else will. Well, they don't want to do it either. So the agency ends up without a Chair at all.

Without adequate leadership, Boards and committees can either become totally useless or fragmented and inappropriately controlling. "Name Only" Chairs are a waste of time; and some groups go out of their way to have Name Only Co-Chairs...two people doing nothing! Looks good on paper...maybe.

HELP!

Most people are reluctant to take on Chair responsibilities because they either don't understand the job or are afraid that they will have to give up their lives to "do it right."

Effective Chairs delegate, lead and inspire...the days of "full time volunteer leadership" are virtually over. It is vital for each Board or group to clarify roles, expectations and make the position as reasonable as possible. How? A unique solution - talk about it!

So Now What?

Throw in the Towel

Hold a Special Meeting

Get Outside Expertise

Clarify Expectations

Celebrate!

Thank Your Board

Clarify Board Roles

Analyze and Recruit

Change Meeting Style

Clarify Terms of Office

Leave Town

Clarify Goals, Objectives

Check Your By-Laws

Just Say No

Just Say Yes

© 1997, Scribner & Associates

WHAT'S IN A NAME?

Being Politically Correct (PC) is not easy, especially regarding nonprofits. Throughout the years we have seen leaders referred to as:

Leaders, Chairman, Chairmen, Chairpersons, Chairpeeps (seen once), Chairwomen, Chairwoman, President, Czar, Czarina...you name it.

Call them what you want - for the purposes of this guidebook all "heads of Boards, committees, groups and states" will be referred to as "Chairs."

By the way, most Boards of Directors and committees refer to their leaders these PC days as "Chairs;" Boards of Trustees tend to have "Presidents." If your organization has a Board of Directors as well as a Board of Trustees, please be kind enough to give the leaders two different titles. Life is confusing enough!

This publication is designed for the Chairs...the ones who often start and end meetings alone...the ones who don't know what hit them when they were elected (that's assuming they were elected). Information regarding Board members, Board/staff relationships, etc. is in many other materials including another Scribner publication, BOARDS FROM HELL. **This one** is for the chosen - the lucky - the few who, like most of us, don't know the difference between a gavel and a hammer.

If you are a Chair, be proud of it. You've joined the ranks of a terrific secret society of others who often suffer in silence. It is now time to "go public;" share the work; orchestrate the crowds; make demands; hold people accountable!

But how?

It's easy. Your greatest ammunition is information...your own and others. Learn the basics of nonprofit law and leadership, and, above all, surround yourself with people who know more than you do and rely upon them. Being a Chair is not about doing all the work - it is about being a fair, honest and consistent leader.

GOOD LEADERS KNOW GOOD WORDS

The most effective Chairs are the ones who embrace three magic words:
"I don't know."

You don't have to be the Universal Answerperson (another PC phrase).

There are a number of sentences that you should repeat, in front of a mirror, until you have them memorized; phrases that can turn a Board funeral into a parade:

"What do you think?" (oooh - this is a tough one, but you can do it)
"Who might have more information about this?"
"Does this need further discussion?"
"What do you believe are our options?"
"Oh, _____ we haven't heard from you about this."

Are you sensing a trend? TO LEAD is "to direct or guide," not serve as a committee or group of one. The key is to involve, let others make decisions (and, yes, mistakes on occasion), give people ownership in both the goals and the work of the group.

If there were to be a banner created for the '90's, it would read:

Good members of Boards, committees and groups do NOT want to witness the work of others. They want their limited time to count. They want their skills to be used. They want their own needs to be met. They want honesty which, for some, means they want out...it is time to clarify roles and expectations for leaders as well as members. It is time to clear the air and start fresh. It is time to learn as well as teach.

GETTING STARTED

1. Have your own assumption party. Grab a garbage bag and a pile of index cards. Write every "rotten" generality or assumption you can think on a separate card. You should be able to write many, many cards. A few of the popular ones include:

> Nobody wants to do anything.
> I get stuck with all the work.
> They don't know enough to make decisions.
> When we joined we were told we didn't have to do anything.
> How can we raise money when there isn't any?
> No one has any time.

Look at each card. REALLY look at each card. Is it a FACT that people don't have time or is your group so boring or flat that people aren't MAKING time? The more "assumptions" we accept, the smaller our universe becomes until we end up working alone. Not much fun. Rip up (and throw out) all nasty assumptions that are keeping you from moving forward. Keep the true ones, i.e. *most people DID join organizations with little or few expectations.* The issue is how to resolve the problems rather than just accept them or let them limit your growth.

This is an exercise that you also should do with your Board or group in private. Bring a BIG bag and a LOT of index cards. Talk about assumptions and issues off the record. You will be amazed at what people are (or are not) thinking that is getting in your way!

Once again, keep the true ones but (literally) take the "garbage" out of the room so you can start with a clean slate!

2. Know what you don't know. Many Chairs are justifiably frightened by what they think they don't know. Nonprofit organizations and groups should be run just like any other type of business, with logic, policies and procedures. There is a tremendous amount of information accessible from finance to legal issues. Similar to learning how to use a computer, however, a Chair does not need to learn ALL of it at once. There are basics of operation to understand and, then, issues and tasks that will necessitate obtaining more information as you move forward.

Make a list of a few major issues that you, personally, wish to learn more about. Perhaps it will include the use of your By-Laws or how to enforce them. Maybe you want to know more about liability insurance (maybe you NEED to know more about liability insurance - ha ha), which brings up a vital issue: LIGHTEN UP ALREADY! You are doing a nice thing. Be gentle with you! Leading a group is a serious job but it doesn't have to be horrible!!!

3. Get a Grip. If you think you're WHOLE GROUP is going to participate equally in all activities, forget it. What you generally will find is about 25% who will be terrific, 50% who just don't have a clue as to what they are doing and another 25% who aren't going to do anything no matter WHAT you do. Forget about the ones who don't want to participate. Embrace those who want to help and talk to, train and focus your energies on that 50% who need guidance and leadership. You will find most of your help there.

4. Know what you want. Everyone needs an exchange, and not necessarily a plaque or a certificate. It is called a WIIFM - What's In It For Me. So, what are YOUR WIIFMs? Do you want to learn something new, gain new skills, use the skills you have, have fun? Unless you know what your own needs are and work with the group toward meeting them, you will constantly be frustrated and unfulfilled. Again, a valuable issue to discuss with each Board or group member individually simply by asking, "if this was a year from now, and you had a great time as a member of this group, WHY?" You may be amazed to find out that your accountant wants to learn public speaking or your marketing person wants to develop programs. Not only do we make unfortunate assumptions about our world, we do so to each other!

19 © 1997, Scribner & Associates

5. Make a plan. Identify your WIIFMS, issues you wish to learn more about, your tasks for the next 12 months and the types of skills with which you would like to be surrounded. Think about how you would best like the group to operate; your expectations of your members and of yourself.

6. Have a meeting with your group. Serve food. Include the group members (and key staff people when appropriate) and conduct the following exercises:

> 1. Assumption Party
> 2. Expectations Exchange
>   What does the group expect from you.
>   What do you expect from the group.
> 3. Outline your personal leadership goals for the year.
> 4. Make arrangements to meet with each member personally to do the same..

GUARANTEED...*your role will instantly change for the better after this exchange!*

WHAT'S MY JOB
(By-Laws vs. My-Laws)

Just because no one else will do it doesn't mean that you have the right to do what you want as the Chair! On the other hand, if you are receiving little or no support, it is not only tempting to do too much, it seems necessary!

Board Chairs, like Boards, are like snowflakes...each is different! Your role will depend a great deal on the needs of the group. Some groups need more guidance than others. No groups need bullies.

The best way to clarify your role is the most simple. Ask your group what they "give you permission to do!" This is an odd, yet effective, way of finding out that your meetings run too long, the group chit chats too much, or individuals feel left out; all of which can be stated nicely without having anything thrown at you.

Most often, when asked what "permission" the group would like to give its Chair, responses will range from "we give you permission to start meetings on time" (which means knock off the chatter at the beginning and get going!), to "we give you permission to keep us on the agenda," a polite way of letting you know that the meeting is jumping all over the place.

An odd thing happens when groups give their leaders permission; they tend to take a more active role in enforcing the new rules. "Hey, we agreed that we would not discuss balloon colors at the Board meetings," reminding the Chair to go ahead and guide the group properly.

One extremely effective (and of course, bizarre) way to involve the group in meeting governance is to appoint an unofficial Sergeant At Arms. This phoney position is best served by a new Board member. Their role? Simply to "enforce" the rules of conduct and permission provided by the group to its Chair. Should someone "break a rule," then the Sergeant can use a variety of tacky techniques at his or her disposal. Favorites include time-out chairs, Stop Whining buttons and the ever popular toe tags to be placed (with names) on members who remain silent during the meeting, obviously having "passed away." Though blatantly silly, these techniques tend to give the group permission to govern itself in a fun and noncombative manner - much more friendly than "Hey, Lois, don't you have a thought in your head?"

There are a few items which appear on most Chair job descriptions. Review them with your volunteer and staff leadership; then include your final version as a matter of record in Board materials. Refer to your By-Laws which usually state next to nothing about the position and expand from there.

CHAIRS OF THE BOARD

- Plan and prepare adequately for meetings (create agendas with staff and member input, ensure that all materials are available)
- Conduct all meetings
- Select and supervise all committee and special group chairs (for Boards)
- Represent the organization to the public (following Board approved policies)
- Assist the agency or group in all fundraising activities (giving a thoughtful gift, helping to obtain the same from members of the group and accompanying staff and volunteers appropriately to meet with prospects)
- Help recruit new volunteers
- Work with the staff leadership to ensure that the agency is meeting all its legal and fiduciary responsibilities
- When applicable, work with other Board members to evaluate the Executive Director
- Ensure that each member of the group or committee receives adequate training, monitoring and evaluation

On Boards, terrific Chairs are "partners" with the leader of the staff. On committees, this partnership is maintained with assigned staff to the group.

The Board Chair is responsible to ensure that the members carry out their functions and conduct themselves properly. "Standards of Conduct" for Board members need to be discussed, put in writing and included as part of a Board information packet.

A fiduciary is an individual having a duty to act for another's benefit. These duties entail the proper utilization, management, or investment of property and other assets placed in their trust. Well meaning persons, whether knowledgeable or not, can fail to manage adequately.

Most By-Laws include a section that states that a Director is not liable for anything except for self-dealing. This, unfortunately, is a misleading spin off of a state code which, in fact, really provides no special protection. It does permit lawsuits alleging that Directors did not perform their duties with the required care or in good faith in the best interests of the corporation. Even though suits may be unfounded (and most are), the issue is that they must be addressed; they must be defended. It is often the cost of defense that represents the greatest risk. Board Chairs should review insurance, state and federal regulations with the agency's counsel in detail. In order to make a "genuine effort" to act in good faith, the Chair is urged to work with the Board to create the following:

> Job descriptions with specific tasks and standards
> Clear expectations that members have of each other
> A system of checks and balances to ensure compliance
> Education and support in such areas as:
> > conducting meetings
> > financial and budgetary preparation, monitoring and implementation
> Professional counsel for the Board
> A system of on-going Board development training

Most agency members have clear definitions of Conflict of Interest, Self-Dealing and other obvious areas of potential problems. In addition to disclosing individual appropriate financial and professional matters, all members of the Board have a legal obligation to disclose potential areas of personal and professional conflict.

Conflict of Commitment can occur when a member of the Board has explicit or implied divided loyalties. For instance, if a member is serving on the Board of an agency which provides medical care and also is serving on a Board which provides immunizations in local neighborhoods, there is a potential conflict of commitment. What does the Board member do when faced with funding information, decisions and program materials?

The best way to address any semblence of Conflict of Commitment is to address it! Very few people work with only one nonprofit! One of the benefits we enjoy in working together is sharing experiences. However, fiduciaries of each nonprofit should be expected to focus their energies where they are at the time! All members should clearly state, in writing, the other nonprofit agencies or organizations with which they play an active role. They should be careful to ensure that when they are meeting with THIS agency, that they are working in its best interest at all times.

Further information about the standards of performance for Board members as well as a sample Board Contracts are included in **BOARDS FROM HELL** (no, this is not a commercial break, but *this* publication is for Chairs!).

UNDERSTANDING BY-LAWS...
WOW! A New Concept!

One of the main roles of the Chair of the Board is to ensure that the organization adheres to its own By-Laws (or Bylaws or BYLAWS or By-laws). This often is easier said than done as most people (other than attorneys) do not truly understand what the By-Laws mean.

A revised set of By-Laws in a new type of format has been developed for this guidebook. It includes "legal-type" articles followed by statements in italics which describe the meaning of each section. Your organization probably needs to update its By-Laws anyway (given new and changing legislation). You may also want to consider developing an additional format for internal use so that all parts of this vital document are understood! The level of explanation needed may vary from person to person and some sections seem obvious on their own. Do not ever underestimate the Board's need for clarification...sometimes too much is not too much. This is one of those times!

© 1997, Scribner & Associates

SAMPLE BY-LAWS FORMAT
"The Agency"
Scribner & Associates

ARTICLE 1
OFFICES

SECTION 1. PRINCIPAL OFFICE
The principal office of the Corporation for the transaction of business is located in
_____.

SECTION 1.
The main office of The Agency is at _____.

SECTION 2. CHANGE OF ADDRESS
The Board of Directors may, however, change the principal office from one location to another by noting the changed address and effective date below, and such changes of address shall not be deemed an amendment of these Bylaws:
_____ Dated: _____

_____ Dated: _____

_____ Dated: _____

SECTION 2.
The Board of Directors of The Agency can change the address of the office from one place to another.

SECTION 3. OTHER OFFICES
The corporation may also have offices at such other places, within or without the State of _____, where it is qualified to do business, as its business may require and as the Board of Directors may, from time to time, designate.

SECTION 3.
The Agency may also have offices at other places, inside or outside of the State of _____ if it is appropriate and necessary.

ARTICLE 2
PURPOSES

SECTION 1. OBJECTIVES AND PURPOSES
The primary objectives for this Corporation shall be to:

AGENCY MISSION STATEMENT PLACED HERE

SECTION 1.
Our goals are to: (list)

ARTICLE 3
DIRECTORS

SECTION 1. NUMBER (OF DIRECTORS)
The Corporation shall have ten (10) to fifteen (15) Directors and collectively the
shall be known as the Board of Directors. The number may be changed by amendment of this Bylaw,
or by repeal of this Bylaw and adoption of a new Bylaw, as provided in these Bylaws.

SECTION 1.
*The Board will have a minimum of 10 Directors and a maximum of 15. The number can be
made higher or lower by vote of the Board.*

SECTION 2. POWERS
Subject to the provisions of the State of _____ Nonprofit Public Benefit Corporation law, the
activities and affairs of this corporation shall be conducted and all corporate powers shall be exercised by or under the direction of the Board of directors.

SECTION 2.
*The State of _____ and the The Agency Bylaws describe the role of the Board of Directors and
what they legally can and cannot do.*

SECTION 3. DUTIES
It shall be the duty of the Directors to:

(a) Perform any and all duties imposed on them collectively or individually
by law, by the Articles of Incorporation of this Corporation, or by these Bylaws;

(b) Appoint and remove, employ and discharge, and, except as otherwise
provided in these Bylaws, prescribe the duties and fix the compensation, if any, of all
officers, agents and employees of the Corporation;

(c) Supervise all officers, agents and employees of the Corporation to
assure that their duties are performed properly;

(d) Meet at such times and places as required by these Bylaws;

(e) Participate in Board training and work with experts from other nonprofit
organizations and others in order to enhance board member effectiveness; and

(f) Register their addresses with the Secretary of the Corporation and
notices of meetings mailed or telegraphed to them at such addresses shall be valid
notices thereof.

SECTION 3.
It's the job of the Directors to:

(a) Implement The Agency 's Bylaws.

(b) Hire and fire people on the Board and anyone who works for pay for The Agency.

*(c) Make sure anybody who is on the Board or who works for pay for The Agency does what
they are supposed to do.*

(d) Meet at the times and places as it stated in these Bylaws.

(e) Go to trainings for all Board members.

(f) Provide the Secretary with current mailing and phone information.

SECTION 4. TERMS OF OFFICE
Directors shall hold office for a period of two (2) years. Elections for Directors shall
be held at the annual meetings as specified in these Bylaws, and a Director shall hold
office until his or her successor is elected and qualifies. After six (6) consecutive

years, or the completion of three (3) full or partial terms of office, whichever is shorter, as a Director, an individual must leave the Board of Directors, and cannot qualify to serve as a Director for at least one full year.

SECTION 4.
People get elected or re-elected for two-year terms at the "annual meeting" each year. Members can only stay on the Board up to 6 years and then they have to take a break for at least one year before they can get elected to the Board again.

SECTION 5. COMPENSATION
Directors shall serve without compensation. They may be allowed reasonable advancement or reimbursement of expenses incurred in the performance of their regular duties as specified in Section 3 of this Article. Directors may not be compensated for rendering services to the Corporation in any capacity other than Director unless such other compensation is reasonable and is allowable under the provisions of Section 6 of this Article.

SECTION 5.
Directors do not get paid for the work they do as Board members. They can get an advance or be paid back for money they spend to be at the meetings or carry out Board duties.

SECTION 6. RESTRICTION REGARDING INTERESTED DIRECTORS

Notwithstanding any other provision of these Bylaws, not more than forty-nine percent (49%) of the persons serving on the board may be interested persons. For purposes of this Section, "interested persons" means either:

(a) Any person currently being compensated by the Corporation for service rendered it within the previous twelve (12) months, whether as a full- or part-time officer or other employee, independent contractor, or otherwise, excluding any reasonable compensation paid to a Director as Director; or
(b) Any brother, sister, ancestor, descendant, spouse, brother-in-law, sister-in-law, son-in-law, daughter-in-law, mother-in-law, or father-in-law of any such person described in subsection (a).

SECTION 6.
Less than half the people serving on the Board of Directors may be what is called an interested person. An "interested person" is:

1. Anyone who was paid by The Agency for some work that they did for The Agency in the last year; or
2. Anyone who is related to someone who was paid by The Agency for some work that they did for The Agency in the last year.

SECTION 7. PLACE OF MEETINGS
Meetings shall be held at the principal office of the Corporation unless otherwise provided by the Board or at such place within or without the State of _____ which has been designated from time to time by resolution of Board of Directors. In the absence of such designation, any meeting not held at the principal office of the Corporation shall be valid only if held on the written consent of all Directors given either before or after the meeting and filed with the Secretary of the Corporation or after all Board members have been given written notice of the meeting as hereinafter provided for special meetings of the board. Any meeting, regular or special, may be

held by conference telephone or similar communications equipment, so long as all Directors participating in the meeting can hear one another.

SECTION 7.
The Agency meetings should be at the office at _____ unless the
Board of Directors decides to hold it somewhere else and puts it in writing.
A meeting can be conducted by phone as long as everyone can hear each other.

SECTION 8. ANNUAL MEETINGS
Annual meetings of Directors shall be held in May.
At the annual meeting of Directors held in May, Directors shall be elected by the Board of Directors in accordance with this section. Cumulative voting by Directors for the election of Directors shall not be permitted. The candidates receiving the highest number of votes up to the number of Directors to be elected shall be elected. Each Director shall cast one vote, with voting being by ballot only.

SECTION 8.
A special once-a-year meeting of the Board of Directors will be in May. It is
called an "Annual Meeting".
At that meeting, Board members, whose terms have expired can be re-elected by the Board of Directors or vacancies of Directors who have left can be filled by new person(s). The persons who get the highest number of votes get to be on the Board. Each Director gets to vote once by a secret ballot.

SECTION 9. SPECIAL MEETINGS
Special meetings of the Board of Directors may be called by the Chair of the Board, the Vice Chair, the Secretary, or by a majority of the Directors, and such meetings shall be held at the place, within or without the State of _____, designated by the person or persons calling the meeting, and in the absence of such designation, at the principal office of the Corporation.

SECTION 9.
Special meetings of the Board of Directors can be called by the Board Chair, Vice Chair, Secretary or any 5 other Directors. Special meetings can be held at the main office or at any other place in the State of _____.

SECTION 10. NOTICE OF MEETINGS
Meetings of the Board shall be held upon four (4) days notice by first-class mail or forty-eight (48) hours notice delivered personally or by telephone. If sent by mail, the notice shall be deemed to be delivered on its deposit in the mail. Such notices shall be addressed to each Director at his or her address as shown on the books of the Corporation. Notice of the time and place of holding an adjourned meeting need not be given to absent Directors if the time and place of the adjourned meeting are fixed at the meeting adjourned and if such adjourned meeting is held no more than forty-eight (48) hours from the time of the original meeting. Notice shall be given of any adjourned regular or special meeting to Directors absent from the original meeting if the adjourned meeting is held more than forty-eight (48) hours from the time of the original meeting.

SECTION 10.
If you hold a meeting of the Board of Directors, you have to notify all members of the Board. You can either send a letter out 4 days before the meeting or tell everyone by phone or in person at least 2 days before the meeting. If you send a letter, the 4 days start as soon as it is mailed. You have to send the letter to the address of the Director as it's written in your official records.

If you start a meeting of the Board and then stop it, if it starts again within 2 days, you don't have to tell Directors who missed the first meeting where the meeting will continue (you can if you want to). If you wait more than 2 days to continue the meeting, then you have to tell **all** *the Directors where and when the meeting will be starting again.*

SECTION 11. CONTENTS OF NOTICE
Notice of meetings not herein dispensed with shall specify the place, day, hour of the meeting and item requiring Board action. The purpose of any Board meeting must be specified in the notice.

SECTION 11.
When a notice is sent about the next Board of Directors meeting (or even made by phone), people must be told what the meeting is about, the date, what time and where it will be.

SECTION 12. MEETING TRANSACTIONS
The transactions of any meeting of the Board, however called and noticed or wherever held, are as valid as though the meeting had been duly held after proper call and notice, provided a quorum, as hereinafter defined, is present and provided that either before or after the meeting each Director not present signs a waiver of notice, a waivers, consents, or approvals shall be filed with the corporate records or made a part of the minutes of the meeting.

SECTION 12.
If you hold a meeting of the Board of Directors and you don't have enough people there for a quorum (see the next section below), then everything accomplished at the meeting is valid as long as people not present sign a paper stating 1. it was acceptable not to get a notice of the meeting; 2. it was acceptable to hold the meeting; or 3. the minutes of the meeting are acceptable. If such documents are signed, they have to be kept with the legal papers of the corporation.

SECTION 13. QUORUM FOR MEETINGS
A quorum shall consist of at least 50% plus one (1) Directors.

Except as otherwise provided in these Bylaws or in the Articles of Incorporation of this Corporation, or by law, no business shall be considered by the Board at any meeting at which a quorum, as hereinafter defined, is not present, and the only motion which the Chair shall entertain at such meeting is a motion to adjourn. However, a majority of the Directors present at such meeting may adjourn from time to time until the time fixed for the next regular meeting of the Board.

When a meeting is adjourned for lack of a quorum, it shall not be necessary to give any notice of the time and place of the adjourned meeting or of the business to be transacted at such meeting, other than by announcement at the meeting at which the adjournment is taken, except as provided in Section 10 of this Article.

The Directors present at a duly called and held meeting at which a quorum is initially present may continue to do business notwithstanding the loss of a quorum at the meeting due to a withdrawal of Directors from the meeting, provided that any action thereafter taken must be approved by at least a majority of the required quorum for such meeting or such greater percentage as may be required by law, or the Articles of Incorporation or Bylaws of this Corporation.

SECTION 13.
To have a legal Board meeting, more than half the Directors must be there or you need to either implement Section 12 or adjourn the meeting.

If you start a meeting with enough Directors and some leave, making it less than 51%, you can keep doing business but you must inform the members who left about what happened later. At least 51% of the Directors must agree with action the Board took.

SECTION 14. MAJORITY ACTION AS BOARD ACTION
Every act or decision done or made by a majority of the Directors present at a meeting duly held at which a quorum is present is the act of the Board of Directors, unless the Articles of Incorporation or Bylaws of this corporation, or provisions of the _____ Nonprofit Public Benefit Corporation Law, particularly those provisions relating to appointment of committees (Section XXXX), approval of contracts or transactions in which a Director has a martial financial interest (Section XXXX) and indemnification of Directors (Section XXXX), require a greater percentage or different voting rules for approval of a matter by the board.

SECTION 14.
If more than half of the Directors are at a meeting, anything they vote on and pass is taken as action of the whole Board, unless something in these bylaws or _____ state laws or other legal papers of the The Agency corporation mandate something different.

SECTION 15. CONDUCT OF MEETINGS
Meetings of the Board of Directors shall be presided over by the Chair of the Board or, if no such person has been so designated or, in his or her absence, the Vice Chair of the corporation or, in the absence of each of these persons, by a Chair chosen by a majority of the Directors present at the meeting. The Secretary of the Corporation shall act as secretary of all meetings of the board, provided that, in his or her absence, the presiding officers shall appoint another person to act as Secretary of the Meeting.

Meetings shall be governed by *Robert's Rules of Order*, and such rules may be revised from time to time, insofar as such rules are not inconsistent with or in conflict with these Bylaws, with the Articles of Incorporation of this Corporation, or with provisions of law.

SECTION 15.
The Chair of the Board will run all Board meetings. If he or she cannot attend, the Vice Chair will do so or a person selected by the group. Robert's Rules of Order will be used to govern the meetings unless the Board adopts a consistent, different manner in which to do so.

SECTION 16. ACTION BY UNANIMOUS WRITTEN CONSENT WITHOUT MEETING

Any action required or permitted to be taken by the Board of Directors under any provision of law may be taken without meeting, if all members of the Board shall individually or collectively consent in writing to such action. For the purposes of this Section only, "all members of the Board" shall not include any "interested Director" as defined in Section XXXX of the _____ Nonprofit Public Benefit Corporation Law Such written consent or consents shall be filed with the minutes of the proceedings of the Board. Such action by written consent shall have the same force and effect as the unanimous vote of the Directors. Any certificate or other document filed under any provision of law which relates to action so taken shall state that the action was taken by unanimous written consent of the Board of Directors without a meeting and that the Bylaws of this Corporation authorize the Directors to so act, and such statement shall be prima facie evidence of such authority.

SECTION 16.
The Board can take action without holding a meeting as long as all of the Directors approve it in writing. Only people who are not "interested" Directors can approve a

Board action by not being at a meeting. "Interested" means people referred to in Article 3, Section 6 as well as any Director who may personally benefit by voting for or against something.

If the Board passes something without holding a meeting, then they have to have it in writing and put it in the Board minutes. Any action that the Board takes this way is just like any action that the Board takes during a meeting.

SECTION 17. VACANCIES

Vacancies on the Board of Directors shall exist (1) on the death, resignation or removal of any Director, and (2) whenever the number of authorized Directors is increased.

The Board of Directors may declare vacant the office of a Director who has been declared of unsound mind by a final order of court, or convicted of a felony, or been found by a final order or judgment of any court to have breached any duty under Section XXXX and following of the _____ Nonprofit Public Benefit Corporation Law.

Directors may be removed without cause by a majority of the Directors then in office. Any Director may resign effective upon giving written notice to the Chair of the Board, the Vice Chair, The Secretary, or the Board of Directors, unless the notice specifies a later time for the effectiveness of such resignation. No director may resign if the Corporation would then be left without a duly elected Director or Directors in charge of its affair, except upon notice to the Attorney General.

Vacancies on the Board may be filed by approval of the Board or, if the number of Directors then in office is less than quorum, by (1) the unanimous written consent of the Directors then in office, (2) the affirmative vote of a majority of the Directors then in office at a meeting held pursuant to notice or waivers of notice complying with this Article of these Bylaws, pr (3) a sole remaining Director.

A person elected to fill a vacancy as provided by this Section shall hold office until the next annual election of the Board of Directors or until his or her death, resignation or removal from office.

SECTION 17.

There are spaces on the Board if one of the Directors dies, resigns or is asked to leave the Board or if the Board changes the Bylaws to state that you want to have more Directors. The Board can ask Directors to leave the Board if; a court states that the person is not stable because of mental health problems; that the Board member has been convicted of a serious crime (felony); or if the member hasn't done what he or she agreed to do as stated in these Bylaws.

A Director can be asked to leave the Board if more than half of the Board vote for him or her to leave.

Any Director can quit the Board as long as they do so in writing and present it to the Chair, Vice Chair, Secretary or the whole Board. Directors can't resign all at the same time unless they notify the Attorney General of the State of _____.

If there is a space on the Board, the Board can fill it. If there are less than 6 Directors on the Board, then they can fill a space only if everyone approves in writing; more than half of the Directors at a legal meeting vote "yes;" or if there is only one Director left.

If someone is chosen to fill someone else's space on the Board, then that person will finish the term of the person who left or until he or she dies, quits the Board or is asked to leave.

SECTION 18. NON-LIABILITY OF DIRECTORS

The Director shall not be personally liable for the debts, liabilities, or other obligations of the corporation.

SECTION 18.
If you are a member of the Board of Directors then you are not usually personally
responsible for the debts as a result of actions by the Board unless you don't take
your Board responsibilities seriously or make every reasonable attempt to
do what is best for The Agency (except for items mentioned in Section XXXX of the _____
Nonprofit law).

SECTION 19. INDEMNIFICATION BY CORPORATION OF DIRECTORS,
OFFICERS, EMPLOYEES AND OTHER AGENTS

To the extent that a person who is, or was, a Director, officer, employee or other agent
of this Corporation has been successful on the merits in defense of any civil, criminal,
administrative or investigation proceeding brought to procure a judgment against such
person by reason of the fact that he or she is, or was, an agent of the corporation, or
has been successful in defense of any claim, issue or matter, therein, such person shall
be indemnified against expenses actually and reasonably incurred by the person in
connection with such proceeding.

If such person either settles any such claim or sustains a judgment against him or her,
then indemnification against expenses, judgments, fines, settlement and other amounts
reasonably incurred in connection with such proceedings shall be provided by this
corporation but only to the extent allowed by, and in accordance with the requirements
of, Section XXXX of the _____ Nonprofit Public Benefit Corporation Law.

SECTION 19.
If you are or used to be a Board member and win or lose a court case
regarding The Agency, you are not personally responsible for paying for
the court costs or fines or other things that might come out of the case (except for
some things that are mentioned Section XXXX of the _____Nonprofit law). If you
lose the lawsuit because you put your own interests ahead of The Agency's interests,
then you may be financially liable.

SECTION 20. INSURANCE FOR CORPORATE AGENTS
The Board of Directors may adopt a resolution authorizing the purchase and
maintenance of insurance on behalf of any agent of the Corporation (including a.
Director, officer, employee or other agent of the corporation) against any liability other
than for violating provisions of law relating to self-dealing (Section XXXX of the
_____ Nonprofit Public Benefit Corporation Law) asserted against or incurred by
the agent in such capacity or arising out of the agent's status as such, whether or not
the Corporation would have the power to indemnify the agent against such liability
under the provisions of Section XXXX of the _____ Nonprofit public Benefit
Corporation Law.

SECTION 20.
The Agency Board of Directors can vote to buy an insurance policy to protect
themselves from most kinds of debts if the corporation gets sued and goes to court.
This insurance will not necessarily protect you if you do not try your best to be a responsible Board
member.

ARTICLE 4
OFFICERS

SECTION 1. NUMBER OF OFFICERS
The officers of the Corporation shall be a Chair, a Secretary, and a Chief Financial
Officer who shall be designated the Treasurer. The Corporation may also have, as
determined by the Board of Directors, a Chair of the Board, one or more Vice
Chairs, Assistant Secretaries, Assistant Treasurers, or other officers. Any number of

offices may be held by the same person except that neither the Secretary nor the Treasurer may serve as the Chair of the Board.

SECTION 1.
The Directors can elect themselves to be the Board officers. People can hold more than one office, but the Secretary and the Treasurer can't serve as the Chair.

SECTION 2. QUALIFICATION, ELECTION, AND TERM OF OFFICE
Any person may serve as officer of this Corporation. Officers shall be elected by the Board of Directors, at any time, and each officer shall hold office until he or she resigns or is removed or is otherwise disqualified to serve, or until his or her successor shall be elected and qualified, whichever occurs first.

SECTION 2.
Anyone can serve as an officer . Officers are elected by the Board of Directors. Officers keep their jobs on the Board until they quit or are asked to leave the Board.

SECTION 3. SUBORDINATE OFFICERS
The Board of Directors may appoint such other officers or agents as it may deem desirable, and such officers shall serve such terms, have such authority, and perform such duties as may be prescribed from time to time by the Board of Directors.

SECTION 3.
The Board of Directors can also choose other officers from time to time if they want.

SECTION 4. REMOVAL AND RESIGNATION
Any officer may be removed, either with or without cause, by the Board of Directors, at any time. Any officer may resign at any time by giving written notice to the Board of Directors or to the Chair or secretary of the Corporation. Any such resignation shall take effect at the date of receipt of such notice or at any later date specified therein, and, unless otherwise specified therein, the acceptance of such resignation shall not be necessary to make it effective. The above provisions of this Section shall be superseded by any conflicting terms of a contract which has been approved or ratified by the board of directors relating to the employment of any officer of the Corporation.

SECTION 4.
The Board of Directors can ask officers to resign their duties at any time. Officers of the Board can resign by notifying the Board in writing.

SECTION 5. VACANCIES
Any vacancy caused by the death, resignation, removal, disqualification, or otherwise, of any officer shall be filled by the Board of Directors. In the event of a vacancy in any office other than that of Chair, such vacancy may be filled temporarily by appointment by the Chair until such time as the Board shall fill the vacancy. Vacancies occurring in offices of officers appointed at the discretion of the Board may or may not be filled as the board shall determine.

SECTION 5.
If someone dies, quits or is asked to resign their officer duties before their time is up, someone else can be chosen by the Board to take their place. The Chair of the Board can also choose someone if they quit between Board meetings. At the next Board meeting, the Board can decide to keep that person or choose someone else.

© 1997, Scribner & Associates

SECTION 6. DUTIES OF THE CHAIR

The Chair shall be the Chief Executive Officer of the Corporation and shall, subject to the control of the Board of Directors, supervise and control the affairs of the Corporation and the activities of the officers. He or she shall perform or issue that all duties are performed incident to his or her office and such other duties as may be required by law, by the Articles of Incorporation of this corporation, or by these Bylaws, or which may be prescribed from time to time by the Board of Directors. Unless another person is specifically appointed as Chair of the Board of Directors, he or she shall preside at all meetings of the Board of Directors. Except as otherwise expressly provided by law, by the Articles of Incorporation, or by these Bylaws, he or she shall, in the name of the Corporation, execute such deeds, mortgages, bond, contracts, checks, or other instruments which may from time to time be authorized by the Board of Directors.

SECTION 6.
The Chair shall be the main executive officer of the Corporation, and supervise the other officers. He or she can sign documents on behalf of The Agency if the Board approves.

SECTION 7. DUTIES OF VICE CHAIR

In the absence of the Chair, or in the event of his or her inability or refusal to act, the Vice Chair shall perform or insure that all the duties of the Chair are performed, and when so acting shall have all the powers of, and be subject to all the restrictions on, the Chair. The Vice Chair shall have other powers and perform such other duties as may be prescribed by law, by the Articles of Incorporation, or by these Bylaws, or as may be prescribed by the Board of Directors.

SECTION 7.
The Vice Chair takes over if the Chair can't or won't do the job.

SECTION 8. DUTIES OF SECRETARY

The Secretary shall:

(a) Certify and keep at the principal office of the Corporation the original, or a copy of these Bylaws as amended or other wise alters to date;

(b) keep at the principal office of the Corporation or at such other places as the board may determine, a book of minutes of all meetings of the Directors, and, if applicable, meeting of committees of Directors, recording therein the time and place of holding, whether regular or special, how called, how notice thereof was given, the names of those present or represented at the meeting, and the proceedings thereof;

(c) See that all notices are duly give in accordance with the provision of these Bylaws or as required by law;

(d) Be custodian of the records and of the seal of the Corporation and see that the seal is affixed to all duly executed documents, the execution of which on behalf of the Corporation under its seals is authorized by law or these Bylaws;

(e) Exhibit at all reasonable times to any Directors of the Corporation, or to his or her agent or attorney, on request therefor, the Bylaws, and the minutes of the proceedings of the Directors of the Corporation; and

(f) In general, perform or cause to be performed all duties incident to the office of Secretary and such other duties as may be required by law, by the Articles of Incorporation of this corporation, or by these Bylaws, or which may be assigned to him or her from time to time by the Board of Directors.

SECTION 8.
The Secretary shall make sure that

      (a) a copy of the Bylaws is kept at the main office
      (b) a book of the minutes of the board and committees is kept at the office
      (c) notices of Board meetings get sent out
      (d) records of the The Agency corporation are kept up
      (e) Directors and appropriate others can inspect the records

SECTION 9. DUTIES OF TREASURER

Subject to the provision of these Bylaws relating to the "Execution of Instruments, Deposits and Funds," the Treasurer shall:

      (a) Have charge and custody of, and be responsible for, all funds and securities of the Corporation, and deposit all such funds in the name of the Corporation in such banks, trust companies, or the depositories as shall be selected by the Board of Directors;

      (b) Receive, and give receipt for, monies due and payable to the corporation from any source whatsoever;

      (c) Disburse, or cause to be disbursed, the funds of the Corporation as may be directed by the Board of Directors, taking proper vouchers for such disbursements;

      (d) Keep and maintain, or cause to be maintained, the adequate and correct accounts of the Corporation's properties and business transactions, including accounts of its assets, liabilities, receipts, disbursements, gain and losses;

      (e) Exhibit at all reasonable times the books of account and financial records to any Director of the Corporation, or to his or her agent or attorney, on request therefor;

      (f) Render to the Chair and Directors, whenever requested, an account of any or all his or her transactions as Treasurer and of the financial condition of the Corporation;

      (g) Prepare, or cause to be prepared, and certify, or cause to be certified, the financial statements to be included in any required reports; and

      (h) In general, perform all duties incident to the office of Treasurer and such other duties as may be required by law, by the Articles of Incorporation of the Corporation, or by these Bylaws, or which may be assigned to him or her from time to time by the Board of Directors.

SECTION 9.
The Treasurer shall make sure that:
      (a) the checking and savings account of the The Agency corporation are kept up to date
      (b) checks as approved by the Board are written
      (c) a report about the The Agency budget is written if asked by the Board
      (d) a report about the budget is given at the board meetings, and
      (e) records are kept up to date so they can be looked at, any time, by
            the Directors or their representatives

ARTICLE 5
COMMITTEES

SECTION 1. EXECUTIVE COMMITTEE

The Board of Directors may, by a majority vote of Directors, designate four (4) or more of its members (who may also be serving as officers of this Corporation) to constitute an Executive Committee and delegate to such Committee any of the powers and authority of the board in the management of the business and affairs of the Corporation, except with respect to:

(a) Filing of vacancies on the Board or on any committee which has the authority of the board;

(b) Fixing of compensation of the Directors for serving on the Board or on any committee

(c) Amendment or repeal of Bylaws or the adoption of new Bylaws

(d) Amendment or repeal or any resolution of the Board which by its express terms is not so amenable or repealable

(e) The appointment of committees of the Board or the members thereof.

(f) Approval of any transaction to which this Corporation is a party and in which one or more of the Directors has a material financial interest, except as expressly provided in Section XXXX of the _____ Nonprofit Public Benefit Corporation Law

By a majority vote of its members then in office, the Board may at any time revoke or modify any or all of the authority so delegated, increase or decrease but not below two (2) the number of its members and fill vacancies therein from the members of the Board. The Executive Committee shall keep regular minutes of its proceedings, cause them to be filed with the corporate records, and report the same to the Board from time to time as the Board may require.

SECTION 1.

The Board of Directors can choose an Executive Committee of four or more people to do Board work. The Executive Committee cannot change the Bylaws, choose people to be on the board, or spend money. If there is an Executive Committee meeting, they have to keep minutes of their meetings and give them to the members at the Board meeting. The Board can change the Executive Committee's membership anytime it wants by vote.

SECTION 2. OTHER COMMITTEES

The Corporation shall have other committees as may from time to time be designated by resolution of the Board of Directors. Such other committees may consist of persons who are not also members of the Board. These additional committees shall act in an advisory capacity only to the Board.

SECTION 2.

The Board of Directors can vote to create other committees. These other committees can include non-Board members along with Board representatives. All committees have no voting rights and serve at the pleasure of the Board.

SECTION 2.1 ADVISORY COUNCIL

There shall be an Advisory Council, appointed by the Board of Directors, consisting of volunteers knowledgeable about The Agency, nonprofit corporations and/or special issues. The Advisory Council shall provide consultation to the Board and help represent The Agency to the public.

SECTION 2.1

The Board will have an "Advisory Council" comprised of professionals in a variety of fields who will provide on-going counsel to the Board and its committees.

SECTION 3. MEETINGS AND ACTION OF COMMITTEES

Meetings and action of committees shall be governed by, notice, held and taken in accordance with the provisions of these Bylaws concerning meetings of the Board of Directors, with such changes in the context of such Bylaws provisions as are necessary to substitute the committee and its members for the Board of Directors and its members, except that the time for regular meetings of committees may be fixed by resolution of the Board of Directors or by the committee. The time for special meetings of committees may also be fixed by the Board of Directors. The Board of

Directors may also adopt rules and regulations pertaining to the conduct of meetings of committees to the extent that such rules and regulations are not inconsistent with the provisions of these Bylaws.

SECTION 3.
Unless the Board adopts special rules for committees, they must use the same rules as the Board to run their meetings.

ARTICLE 6
MEMBERS

SECTION 1. MEMBERS AND MEMBERSHIP
Nothing in these Bylaws shall be construed as limiting the right of the Corporation to refer to persons associated with it, who participate in activities of the Corporation, as "members" even though such persons are not Members as defined in section XXXX of the State of _____ Corporations Code. Such persons shall be deemed to be associated persons with respect to the Corporation as that term is defined in section XXXX of the _____ Nonprofit Public Benefit Corporation Law and no such reference shall constitute anyone a member of this Corporation.

SECTION 1.
The Agency can call anyone who participates in its activities a "member" but those "members" don't have any legal rights to run the Corporation.

ARTICLE 7
EXECUTION OF INSTRUMENTS, DEPOSITS AND FUNDS

SECTION 1. EXECUTION OF INSTRUMENT
The Board of Directors, except as otherwise provided in these Bylaws, may by resolution authorize any officer or agent of the Corporation to enter into any contract or execute and deliver any instrument in the name of and on behalf of the Corporation, and such authority may be general or confined to specific instances. Unless so authorized, no officer, agent, or employee shall have any power or authority to bind the corporation by any contract or engagement or to pledge its credit or to render it liable monetarily for any purpose or in any amount.

SECTION 1.
The Board of Directors can choose someone to represent the corporation and sign contracts or speak for them. If these contracts have something in them about money or credit, the Board has to approve them.

SECTION 2. CHECKS AND NOTES
Except as otherwise specifically determined by resolution of the Board of Directors, or as otherwise required by law, checks, draft, promissory notes, orders for the payment of money, and other evidence of indebtedness of the Corporation shall be signed by the Treasurer and countersigned by the Chair of the Corporation.

SECTION 2.
If the corporation maintains a checking account, the Treasurer and the Chair of the Board of Directors have to sign the checks .

SECTION 3. DEPOSIT
All funds of the Corporation shall be deposited from time to time to the credit of the Corporation in such banks, trust companies, or other depositories as the Board of Directors may select.

SECTION 3.
The Agency must maintain its own bank account.

SECTION 4. GIFTS
The Board of Directors may accept on behalf of the Corporation Any contribution, gift
bequest, or devise for the charitable or public purpose of this Corporation.

SECTION 4.
The Board of Directors can accept contributions or gifts if they are for use as stated in the Bylaws
(Article 2, Section 1).

ARTICLE 8
CORPORATE RECORDS, REPORTS AND SEAL

SECTION 1. MAINTENANCE OF CORPORATE RECORDS
The Corporation shall keep at its principal office in the State of _____;
    (a) Minutes of all meetings of Directors, committee of the Board
indicating the time and place of holding such meetings, whether regular or special,
how called, the notice given, and the names of those present and the proceedings
thereof;
    (b) Adequate and correct books and records of accounts, including accounts of its properties
and business transactions and accounts of it assets, liabilities,
receipts, disbursements, gains and losses; and
    (c) A copy of the Corporation's Articles of Incorporation and Bylaws as
amended to date.

SECTION 1.
At the main office of the Corporation, The Agency must keep a copy of the Articles of Incorporation, the
minutes of the Board meetings; records of the money received, spent or owed; and a copy of the most
current Bylaws.

SECTION 2. CORPORATE SEAL
The Board of Directors may adopt, and use at will, a corporate seal. Such seal
shall be kept at the principal office of the Corporation. Failure to affix the seal to
Corporate instruments, however, shall not affect the validity of any such instrument.

SECTION 2.
The Board can have a special metal stamp to use on business papers but does not
have to use it in order to make papers legal. It must be kept at the main office.

SECTION 3. DIRECTORS' INSPECTION RIGHTS
Every Director shall have the absolute right at any reasonable time to inspect and copy
all books, records and documents of every kind and to inspect the physical properties
of the Corporation.

SECTION 3.
Board members can look at and make copies of the official agency materials,
papers, books, records and property at any reasonable time if it is for The Agency's
business.

SECTION 4. RIGHT TO COPY AND MAKE EXTRACT
Any inspection under the provisions of this Article may be made in person or by agent
or attorney and the right to inspection includes the right to copy and make extracts.

SECTION 4.
Board members can have other people look at and copy the official records for them.

SECTION 5. ANNUAL REPORT
The Board shall cause an annual report to be furnished not later than one hundred and twenty (120) days after the close of the Corporation's fiscal year to all Directors of the Corporation and, if this Corporation has members, to any member who request it in writing, which report shall contain the following information in appropriate detail:

(a) The assets and liabilities, including the trust funds, of the Corporations of the end of the fiscal year;

(b) The principal changes in assets and liabilities, including trust funds, during the fiscal year;

(c) The revenue or receipts of the Corporation, both unrestricted and restricted to particular purposes, for the fiscal year; and

(d) The expenses or disbursements of the Corporation, for both general and restricted purposes, during the fiscal year;

The annual report shall be accompanied by any report thereon of independent accountants, or, if there is no such report, the certificate of an authorized officer of the Corporation that such statements were prepared without audit from the books and records of the Corporation.

SECTION 5.
The Corporation has to prepare a report each year, by the end of _____. The report must provide details about the money the Corporation received, spent and owes for that year. It is advised to get an accountant to look at (audit) the report to verify it. If an audit is not conducted, an officer of the Corporation must sign a document stating that the Annual Report was written without an "audit".

ARTICLE 9
FISCAL YEAR

SECTION 1. FISCAL YEAR OF THE CORPORATION
The fiscal year of the Corporation shall begin on the first day of July and end on the last day of June in each year.

SECTION 1.
Rather than using a "calendar year," The Agency's official year will go from July 1 through June 31 each year. This is common with corporations.

ARTICLE 10
AMENDMENT OF BYLAWS

SECTION 1. AMENDMENT
Subject to any provision of law applicable to the amendment of Bylaws, of public benefit nonprofit corporations, these Bylaws, or any of them, may be altered, amended or repealed and new Bylaws adopted by approval of the Board of Directors.

SECTION 1.
These Bylaws can be changed by the Board of Directors. If they are changed it is advised to send a copy to the State Attorney General.

ARTICLE 11
AMENDMENT OF ARTICLES

SECTION 1. AMENDMENT OF ARTICLES
Any amendment of the Articles of Incorporation may be adopted by approval of the Board of Directors.

© 1997, Scribner & Associates

SECTION 1.

The Articles of Incorporation can be changed by the Board of Directors. If they are changed, the Board must send any changes to the Secretary of State and the federal IRS.

SECTION 2. AMENDMENTS REGARDING INITIAL DIRECTORS AND INITIAL AGENT FOR SERVICE OF PROCESS

This Corporation shall not amend its Article of Incorporation to alter any statement which appears in the original Articles of Incorporation regarding initial Directors or initial agent for service of process except to correct an error or delete such reference only after the Corporation has filed a "Statement by a Domestic Non-Profit Corporation" pursuant to section XXXX of the _____ Nonprofit Corporation Law"

SECTION 2.

The Board cannnot change the original Articles of Incorporation or the names of the very first Board members listed, unless there were a mistake. Documents must be prepared according to Section XXXX of the State of _____ Nonprofit Laws.

ARTICLE 12
PROHIBITION AGAINST SHARING CORPORATE PROFITS AND ASSETS

SECTION 1. PROHIBITION AGAINST SHARING CORPORATE PROFITS AND ASSETS

No Director, officer, employee, or other person connected with this Corporation, or any private individual, shall receive at any time of the net earnings or pecuniary profit from the operations of the Corporation, provided, however, that this provision shall not prevent payment to any such person or reasonable compensation for services performed for the corporation in effecting any of its public or charitable purposes, provided that such compensation is otherwise permitted by these Bylaws and is fixed by resolution of the Board of Directors; and no such person or persons shall be entitled to share in the distribution of, and shall not receive any of the corporate assets on dissolution of the corporation.

SECTION 1.

While the Corporation can pay people for things they do and reimburse their expenses, The Agency can't give Board members, employees or other people extra money left over in the account. If - for any reason - The Agency dissolves, the money and property of the Corporation must be given to another nonprofit or charity. No Board member, person or employee can have any remaining assets.

PARLIAMENTARY PROCEDURES
How to Conduct Non-Deadly Meetings

ROBERT'S RULES OF ORDER...brrrrr

I hate *Robert's Rules*. I never met Mr. Robert, but he has played a major role in my life. His *Rules of Order* drive me crazy. I know, I know, without rules our meetings would be more chaotic than they already are (THERE'S a horrible thought).

Believe it or not, there are those among us who are professional parliamentarians. Hmmm. I bet THEY'RE fun at a party... "USE THE COASTER," "THE SMALL FORK GOES ON THE LEFT SIDE." No doubt they are great at keeping bowling scores and remembering who has which cards in bridge.

Actually, most parliamentarians are pretty neat people; they just want to help us keep organized and out of trouble. But the trouble is that there aren't enough of them to go around. SO, when someone in the room is in the least familiar with the rules, THEY WIN.

Some groups spend more time on rules than they do on business. That's where I draw the line. Have you READ *Robert's Rules*? Now, THERE'S a snooze to remember.

Good old Henry Martyn Robert (born in 1837 and still living for all I know) graduated from West Point and defended Washington D.C. during the Civil War. Like others of us from that area, Henry decided to create his own rules. He apparently felt that two-thirds was better than one-half in most situations.

General Robert had a field day creating his own rules ranging from "members not present are considered to be voting "yes"," that "speeches are limited to ten minutes," (too bad we lost that one) and that "any member can speak only twice during a debate" (wouldn't THAT shorten Board meetings).

Millions of copies of *Robert's Rules of Order* (in more than ten editions) have been published (second in sales only to the *Bible*). His theories serve as the basis for more than 200 titles on the subject written by such notables as a sociologist, a psychiatrist, a veterinarian (I'd like a copy of that one), a priest and a nun among others. Wow, what a library you could have.

AND HE WASN'T ALONE

Actually, Thomas Jefferson wrote the first American manual of parliamentary law which he cleverly named "Jefferson's Manual." After Jefferson, a whole bunch of people started fooling with the procedures, especially lawyers. Luther Cushing wrote the first work on this topic for nonlegislative groups in 1856. Rufus Waples and Thomas Reed in 1883 and 1894 followed suit with quite popular results. Then General Robert came along.

Members of the judiciary, organizations and individuals were very critical of Robert's hard efforts. A number of people wrote revised rules; using legal case law and more modern terms. The most widely used of these include Joseph O'Brien's *Parliamentary Law for the Layman*, Marguerite Grummie's *Basic Principles of Parliamentary Law and Protocol* and Henry Davidson, M.D.'s *Handbook for Parliamentary Practice*. And, of course, we have *Robert's Rules of Order Revised*, *Robert's Rules of Order Newly Revised* and, no doubt, a revision of the revision in process.

New versions of parliamentary procedures are in the works all the time. Board leaders are advised to keep abreast of these changes as:

courts rely heavily on agency bylaws and ordinary custom and usage of parliamentary procedure. Robert's Rules of Order is not always binding...

Many states have adopted parliamentary procedure codes and sections that were formerly covered by the "master" rules of parliamentary procedure. The Board is obligated to ensure that the agency adopt a set of laws - a contract - among itself as to how it will be governed. Chairs are encouraged to obtain their own state's regulations and contact the National Association of Parliamentarians (which has a nifty quarterly publication about this issue), a wide variety of instruction programs and undoubtedly enjoyable social gatherings! Also, check out your local library, the League of Women Voters, Meeting Professionals International, Toastmasters, the American Society of Executives, Volunteer Centers, Support Centers, Centers for Nonprofit Management, the National Center for Nonprofit Boards and a cross section of other nonprofit organizations' policies and procedures. No need to reinvent this already reinvented wheel!

HOW LONG SHOULD MEETINGS TAKE?

This is not a race. Meeting should take as long as they need to take, but any meeting longer than two hours is borderline suicide for most people. Morning meetings *tend* to go faster than evening ones. If people are going to lie they usually will do so at night because they are too tired to fight about anything or admit they cannot perform an expected job.

ISN'T IT EASIER IF THE EXECUTIVE COMMITTEE HANDLES ALL ISSUES?

One of the major reasons that Boards become dysfunctional is that well meaning Executive Committees handle all the affairs, systematically removing any semblence of ownership on the part of the rest of the Board. Comments such as "why should I be here; it doesn't matter" are frequently heard from Board members who are not part of Executive Committees.

Easy rule to follow: check your By-Laws regarding the purpose of your Executive Committee. Count on the fact that you are probably out of compliance anyway. If you are not a national organization or cannot come up with a TERRIFIC reason to have an Executive Committee, get rid of it (except for issues of fiduciary concerns, true emergencies and Executive Director evaluations). Chances are that, if you have an Executive Committee, you are really operating with a Board of four and a bunch of witnesses. Not a very strong team.

WHO SHOULD ATTEND MEETINGS?

Obviously, all Board members and the Executive Director should attend all Board meetings. Appropriate staff should be invited to attend as needed (having staff members "outline the room sitting on chairs" is not a good use of agency skills). Each committee should have a staff representative serving on it. "Executive Sessions" are special meetings for voting members of the Board only. They can be "called" for special issues such as the Executive Director's performance review, personnel matters, certain financial activities and other internal issues which need private discussion.

AND IN THE MEANTIME...

The following pages include a few samples of BASIC Parliamentary Procedures which may be helpful as you and your volunteer and staff leadership review your own policies. A sample script of "basic meeting jargon" also is included! Following the examples, there are some tips regarding effective ways to RUN a meeting. Whether you use *Robert's Rules* or not, SOMEBODY has to keep things moving along or you may find yourself meeting alone!

43 © 1997, Scribner & Associates

TYPES OF AGENDAS

1. Action focus
    - each subject area listed
    - columns checked
        - for discussion only
        - for Board action
        - for referral to committee
2. Timed
    8:00 - 8:12 Introductions
    8:12 - 8:15 Approve minutes
    Etc.
3. Deadly
    wing it

ONE HECK OF AN AGENDA:

I. Welcome
    A. Call to Order
    B. Roll Call (names are checked present, not present)
    C. Introduction of guests

II. Ratification of Minutes of Previous Meeting
    (a motion is required for this)

III. Approval of agenda
    (a motion is required for this too - but it gives everyone a chance to glance over the agenda and add issues they want discussed)

IV. Reports
    (committee chairs are asked to keep their reports to a maximum of five minutes)
    Program
    Finance
    Membership
    Development
    Public Relations
    other

V. Executive Director's Report (another short presentation)

VI. Unfinished business
    New items are identified and some disposition is made by the Board (refer to committee, etc.)

VII. Information Items (again, five minutes on various topics of importance raised by the Board)

VIII. New Business

IX. Announcements

X. Adjournment (motion and vote required)

XI. Executive Session (if required)

© 1997, Scribner & Associates

HARMLESS PARLIAMENTARY PROCEDURE NOTES

Conducting an effective meeting should not be a traumatic experience.

- **Call to order (start the meeting, noting the time).**
    Call the meeting to order at the exact time it was scheduled to start. Even if no one is there. Next time, they may show up! The meeting also should end on time. If more time is necessary than planned, the group should agree to continue; however the Chair should acknowledge that the ending time has occurred.
- **Ask that the minutes of the last meeting be approved as received and read (!) by the members.** If there are no changes, the minutes can stand approved as read by Board vote.
- **Officer reports, standing committee reports.** Any special recommendations should be dealt with as motions. It would be helpful if the Board knows how to read the budget! This is a rare occurance. It usually is the Treasurer (a CPA elected for life) who is the only one in the room who understands the reports. Watch what happens when Board members are asked if there are any questions.... talk about silence!
- **Special committee reports.**
- **Executive Director report.** The placement of this important report varies with different nonprofit agencies. Many agencies put it first. It is felt that this turns the meeting into a staff driven production rather than a Board meeting.
- **Unfinished business.** This is all the stuff no one remembered to talk about or the committee Chairs left out.
    This is not the time to discusss what color the invitation should be for the special event. That belongs in a committee.
- **New businesss.** The Chair should ask if there is any. There usually isn't.
- **Announcements**: When's the next party, who sold the most tickets, other fun things.
- **Adjournment.** On time. Vote to end the meeting after making sure there is no further business to discuss.

45   © 1997, Scribner & Associates

BOB'S RULES OF DISORDER

1. Start the meeting on time
     (call to order)

2. Approve minutes from last time
     (read them for the first time)

3. Standing Committee reports
     (seated, too - summaries please)

4. Whoops report
     (unfinished business)

5. What new mess is this
     (new business)

6. The inside scoop
     (executive staff report)

7. Tell it like it is
     (announcements)

8. Don't let the door hit you on the way out
     (adjournment)

MOTION SICKNESS

There are many ways to make motions. There are many types of motions. Ponder these instructions from basic parliamentary procedures:

"If you want to amend an amendment, the first vote is on the amendment to the amendment either as changed or as originally proposed, depending on the first vote. The second vote is on the first amendmendment either as changed or as originally proposed, depending on the first vote. The third vote is on the main motion either as introduced or as amended."

There must be an easier way to get through these meetings...

There is. Talk about procedures before you conduct meetings!

What is a motion? How should motions be worded, presented, used? Motions generally are "focused directives;" they should set policies, platforms or state an action to be taken. Many organizations present and pass motions that really didn't need to be made in the first place. Ask a series of questions about each motion such as:

"Why are we taking this action or making this motion?"
"Is the motion already part of our agency's mission or programs?"
"Is it legal? Is it appropriate?"
"How does it fit our mission, values, goals and objectives?"
"Is it specific...what are we going to DO as a result of its approval?"
"What will happen if we don't approve it?"
"Does it include assignments and expectations of Board or staff?"

It truly helps to send "draft motions" ahead to the members of the group when possible, giving people ample time to review them. Keep in mind that many people may not understand the content, intent or ramifications of motions they approve...and few people will admit to this. Motions sent ahead on a form that addresses the questions above tend to be most easily understood.

There are issues of points of order, appeals, questions, and inquiries. YOUR Board or group needs to clarify how **it** is going to introduce motions, discuss issues and vote on them. Following *Robert's Rules of Order* in general is a fine way to go; only if *everyone* is following the same rules.

© 1997, Scribner & Associates

A MUCH REQUESTED SAMPLE SCRIPT...I SECOND THATEE MOTION...

(Be sure to check *Robert's Rules* or other sources of parliamentary procedure before adopting your rules. This is an abbreviated version of what you may expect!)

"Mr./Madam Chair." *(Board member)*

"Yes, (name of member)?" *(Chair)*

"I move that....." *(Board member states the motion)*

"I second the motion." *(another Board member)*

"It has been moved and seconded that (repeat the motion). Is there any discussion?" *(Chair)*

"Yack yack yack." *(Board)* Discussion on the stated motion begins. During this time, member(s) may offer a "substitute motion," replacing the first. If so, record the substitute (which needs a second and a vote) and continue the discussion. Others may wish to add a "friendly ammendment" to the motion under discussion. Record this ammendment (with a second and a vote) and continue discussion on the revised motion (if approved).

"I call for the question." *(Board member wanting the yacking to stop)* Requires a second and a vote.

"The question is on the motion (repeat the motion). Those in favor, state (or stand or raise a hand) "Aye." Pause. "All opposed, "No." *(Chair)*

Sometimes new motions may be made to
- **Extend the Discussion** for a limited period of time (requires a second and a vote and is not debatable).
- **Refer the Motion to a Committee** for further study (requires a second and a vote).
- **Postpone the Motion Indefinitely** (truly meant to kill the motion; requires a second and a vote and is debatable).
- **Withdraw the Motion** (by the author) After the motion has been stated by the Chair, it only can be withdrawn by general consent or a vote.

If the members approve to go ahead and vote, repeat the motion and vote on it. Don't forget to ask for and record abstentions. Announce results (carried, defeated). *(Chair)* At certain times you may wish to record each vote by individual name or exact count. Anyone can request this for the record.

When finished, move, second and vote to end the meeting. Then prepare the minutes!

© 1997, Scribner & Associates

SIXTY SECOND MINUTES

Two sounds tend to bring out the worst in good volunteers and staff members; one is the tick tick tick of metal knitting needles during a meeting and the other, more annoying, is the sound of envelopes being ripped open for the first time when the Chair asks to review the minutes or reports that had been SENT AHEAD BECAUSE PEOPLE COMPLAINED. Augh!

We all have seen minutes that go on and on and on and on...small wonder that few people review the whole packet. Upon arrival at the meeting, members are encouraged (at the very least) to open the packet in their cars, ruffle the papers a bit and, for the ultimate, use a highlighter on a few lines. At least people will think you READ the information!

Better yet, why not make the information easier to review? There are few exceptions to the ability to use uniform committee or group report formats. Board minutes should not include a blow by blow account of each word said however breathtaking it may seem at the time. A few basic rules may help encourage members to both send in reports and read them! **Remember: Record what was done, NOT what was said.**

1. First paragraph
    Type of meeting (special, etc)
    Time, date, place
    Members, staff and guests present
    Chair and Secretary names
    Motion, discussion and vote regarding previous minutes

2. Body of Minutes
    Separate paragraph for each subject matter
    • names of motion movers and exact motion wording
    • names of seconds
    • results

3. Last paragraph
    Time of adjournment
    Next meeting date, location and time

4. Signed by the Secretary

Note the "Signed by the Secretary" rule. Official Board (and at times committee) Secretaries often are not able to participate in meetings due to the fact that their time is spent taking notes. Boards in particular are encouraged to have a professional secretary in the room to record the meeting and then review the material with the Secretary for approval and signature before distribution.

© 1997, Scribner & Associates

MINI COMMITTEE REPORTS

Picture it - five committees, five one-page reports...makes you want to swoon, eh? Well, it's possible! Why not have your own version of a uniform report format for committee and/or special reports, limited as much as possible to one page (plus appropriate attachments)...

Committee Report

Committee:

Board liaison:

Chair:

Members:

Report for the month of:

Fiscal report: Income, expenditures, balance

Three most important items you accomplished:

Three items you plan for next month:

What you expect from the Board/staff to do so:

Board action required for this meeting (attach copy of the motion draft)

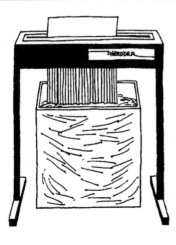

© 1997, Scribner & Associates

MEETING MANDATES...
AND ADD YOUR OWN!

1. Vote of majority decides (some use consensus instead)

2. All members have equal rights

3. Minority opinions must be heard

4. Full and free discussions should be encouraged

5. Only one motion should be considered at at time

6. Every member should clearly understand the motion

7. Anyone, any time should feel free to ask a question

8. Always have food

9. Schedule consistent dates, times, yet be flexible to members

10. Change the meeting site once in a while

11. Include staff appropriately

12. Have a party - Board and staff

13. Don't distance yourself from your clients

14. Remember the privilege is serious...

15. Know your own needs and limitations

16. Let yourselves have fun

17. Keep members on track...no whispering, needlepoint or newspapers

18. Chairs should keep personal ideas and thoughts to an absolute minimum - as a member of the group, not the sole source of information. Let the group make decisions. The Chair generally should not vote unless by ballot or to cast the deciding vote on an issue...always a popular position to maintain

19. Instead of Board Retreats have Board *Advances*

© 1997, Scribner & Associates

LONELY AT THE TOP
Getting Others to Help

Poor Chair...So often, happy members of the group find themselves becoming isolated, scorned, blamed and nagged because they agreed (usually reluctantly) to accept The Gavel. Sigh. Why did this dream turn into a nightmare?

Because you are a sucker!

Face it. The more you give, the more they'll take. Why? Because THEY DON'T KNOW WHAT YOUR JOB IS EITHER!! Why do you think no one else wanted to do this?

Beyond the crazy characters outlined in the front of this guidebook, there seem to be two basic types of true "chairs" -

Those who are sat upon and those who stand alone.

These two extremes go from having all the volunteers, board members, staff, donors and clients sitting on your lap, to no one working with you at all.

Both extremes are lousy. How about something in between?

Imagine, if you will, Chair Heaven:

Clear role and responsibility
Limited hours of commitment
Expertise at your fingertips
Functioning committees
   (think hard on that one)
Meetings starting & stopping
   on time
Members knowing their roles
And OH -
OTHERS DOING MORE!

STOP TEASING ME, I CAN'T TAKE IT!

Hey - no tease. No fooling. You, too, can have a life. This road can be a lot more easily traveled. Back to the key word - information!

Wonder why you get so many calls? People need help and guidance.
or
Wonder why no one calls? They don't know how to use leadership.

Either way, it's up to you to institute a number of processes which will help others help themselves, support you and each other and, most of all, use their skills and energy most appropriately to do what is best for your clients. And that's where it all starts. Clients.

When is the last time you visited with the people you serve - those whom you are privileged to champion; those who are relying upon your voice, your heart, your words, to do what is right for them?

Dysfunction (and nonfunction for that matter) on a Board often comes from a lack of emotion. Sounds sappy, but it's true. If you are mad, you will work. If you are excited, you will work. Determined. Hopeful. Focused.

Focused. Key word. All roads in nonprofit management success do not lead to paper trails...they lead to clients. People...animals...the environment in which we live...the preservation of our cultures and arts. Something that is bigger and more important than we are. Others' needs.

Strangely enough, your most important ammunition has been there all along - your clients.

"What does our group need to do...for our clients?"
"What tasks must we achieve...for our clients?"
"What skills do we need to do our tasks...for our clients?"
"How much money must we raise...for our clients?"

Your agency's plan, your group's vision for its clients, is your most important tool in bringing energy and life to you and your Board. If you are focused and ex- cited about the possibilities, you will reach out. If you are focused, you will find new energy.

If you are doing a job because you have to, don't even bother. Let your Board resign and get out of the way so that another group can take over. Is it that easy? Yes. There is no question that if your group disappears another will take its place. This is not about the preservation of your organization. It is about clients and what is best for them.

SO, assuming you'd like to reach for that dream...

53   © 1997, Scribner & Associates

GET YOUR MEMBERS FOCUSED AND ON TRACK

1. Conduct the assumption party mentioned previously.
2. Remember to meet with each member individually to discuss WIIFMS.
3. Spend a meeting talking about your clients. If appropriate, visit with them on a regular or special basis.
   - Why is each member interested?
   - Why this group and not another?
   - What solutions are offered here that are special?
   - What would happen if our solutions were not available?
4. Review your strategic plan. If you don't have one, create one with the group. It's not hard to do and is the most important gift you can provide.

   The first part of your plan should detail the next 2-3 years and contain a wish list for future ideas. The second part of your plan should address how your agency intends to pay for the first part! Ah, fundraising!

It is vital that all Board members, key staff and volunteers participate in the process of planning. Again, your greatest tool. Information. Make sure it is their plan, not yours, not the staff's nor some committee's.

> *People give the most of their time, talent, and funds where they are the most involved. There is no greater level of ownership than to be among the creators of a vision.*

BASED ON YOUR VISION, IDENTIFY SPECIFIC, NEEDED TASKS

Define every task you can think of. Do not worry whether it is a "staff" or "volunteer" job. This is a partnership...

DISCUSS ROLES OF BOARD AND STAFF FOR EACH TASK

Examine each task in detail:
- What are the specific outcomes we wish to achieve?
- What are the action steps necessary to achieve them?
- What is the staff's responsibility? The Board's? The Chair's?

 AH HA! NOW YOU CAN TALK ABOUT THE GAVEL!

© 1997, Scribner & Associates

CLARIFY THE ROLE OF THE BOARD

CLARIFY THE ROLE OF THE CHAIR OF THE BOARD

SWAP EXPECTATIONS OF EACH OTHER

**DISCUSS THE ROLE AND EXPECTATIONS OF
    AND BY THE STAFF WITH THE BOARD**

PROVIDE MEMBERS WITH HELPFUL PACKETS
    Rules, laws, By-laws, the budget, etc.

Fasten your Chair Belt... here come's the big one:

DISCUSS STRUCTURE! OH NO! OH YES!!

Wipe out all your committees. You can do it. Zap. They are gone. And, yes, even that nasty Executive Committee. Bye.

NOW - with your Board and key staff, look at your To Do list:
    What committees do you REALLY need (the fewer the better)?
    What is each committee's purpose? Goals? Objectives? Workplans?
        Watch this one - it's the one I always fall for:
            "Should a Board member Chair the Committee? Yes?"
            "Well it seems that the Committee Chair needs to
            make sure that all these plan are carried out; that
            everyone will do their tasks. So, who will agree
            to temporarily orchestrate this committee as it grows?
        *This really helps recruit a Chair - why? Because the job is
        clear, the goals are set, the workplans are identified and
        their job ALSO is to delegate - just like YOURS!*
    What should we expect of Committee Chairs? Them of us?
    What skills do we need on this committee?
    Where can we find them (they probably aren't on the Board,
        no offense) - to soften that blow you can remind people
        that committees are a GREAT recruiting tool for new
        talent and expertise for the Board (whew).
    What process should we use to recruit new people (ah, I
        hear a Nominating Committee in the works).

*hmmm...somebody's job is starting to get
a bit more humane!*

IF YOU AND YOUR BOARD NEED TO:

Review your By-Laws (line by line)
Review all your insurance policies and agency documents
Approve your job descriptions
Change your meeting dates/times
Throw a pie - make a change once in a while
Learn what to look for in a budget or financial statement
Ensure all your disclosures are disclosed
Get training in areas such as public relations, speaking, fundraising and other needed areas

Give each other permission to NOT KNOW EVERYTHING. Then, together, you can learn with enthusiasm. No more tears learning!

Ten minutes of each Board or committee meeting should focus on "yet another aspect of this wonderful job of ours." A new topic each time ranging from client needs and services to how to handle reporters who call. Constant training and support.

OH YE OF LITTLE FAITH...SOME THOUGHTS ON DELEGATION

"They won't do it," is a nasty, unfair assumption. Toss it or don't bother trying. Stop whining. Also check your attitude (ahem)...are you SURE you want to delegate? Is it okay for others to make mistakes? Do you really think you are the only one who cares? If you are a perfection freak this is a terrific exercise in reality. Think about it.

Why should you delegate:

To save your skills for most important issues.
To help others gain new skills and understanding.
To use everyone's time effectively.

What should you delegate:

Routine tasks to start with.
Anything that someone else is anxious to learn how to do.
Anything that someone else already knows how to do.
Activities which already are detailed and ready to be done.
Brainstorming. The most important thing to delegate - let others cut loose and have fun creating options for the group's consideration.

Think about the benefits of delegating:

How you will feel. How it can make others feel.
How you can use the time better. How others can make a difference.
How this will make your job more reasonable!

© 1997, Scribner & Associates

THE BUSINESS OF THE BOARD

FINANCE - TRUSTEESHIP

Planning is great fun. Creating values is terrific. Doing great things for great people is a joy. Nonprofits, however, also are businesses and need to be treated as such!

One of the most important responsibilities of Boards is trusteeship. Safeguarding shareholders assets is how private organizations do so. Although nonprofit organizations do not have stockholders, we have similar responsibilities.

This trusteeship includes services to both the funding sources and the community; accountability of programs and accounting for budgetary techniques; proper financial planning and investing of excess funds. During the past few years organizations many have been creating endowments. similar to sophisticated savings accounts. Though in the past these "savings accounts" were considered risky ("they already have money, what do they need ours for?"), there is no question that zero based budgeting is a thing of the past. Donors are attracted to a well run, future-minded and financially stable organization. Planned Giving (money from dead people) is one of the fastest growing funding methods.

Financial Policies should include the following:
    Methods of Accounting
    Annual Budget (timing and format)
    Segregation of Duties (how and when revenues are deposited)
    Staff and Volunteer Reimbursement policies
    Dual Signatures Provisions
    Record Retention Systems (and safeguarding procedures)
    Solicitation and Gifts policies (what you will/will not accept)
    Contract, Leases and Loan Policies (who signs, who approves)
    Directors and Officers Insurance
    Regular Financial Reporting to the Board
        Current Balance Sheet
        Year to Date Profit and Loss Statements
        Report of reimbursements
        Contracts, leases and loans for approval
        List of cash and non-cash receipts
        List of cash disbursements
        Risk management issues
        Annual budget

Count on the fact that the majority of your Board members do not know what to look for on your financial reports. Teach them how to ask appropriate questions!

OTHER POLICIES AND PROCEDURES

The Chair is responsible to ensure that the Board discusses and adopts policies and procedures. Policies are rules for organizational behavior; statements of authority, values, procedures of how things will be done within the agency. Procedures give us consistency.

In addition to areas of finance, policies are needed in:

- program scope and objectives
- general organization and procedures of agency and Board operation
- defining the management areas of staff
- personnel relations and procedures
- public relations, information distribution
- financial development

Policies should be:

- developed by Board or Board committees with staff input
- written
- approved by the Board
- distributed to all appropriate people

BOARD MEMBER RIGHTS (DO WE DARE SAY 'OBLIGATIONS'?)

Attending a meeting every month or every other month does not a good Board member make. Advisory Councils are wonderful places for individuals who wish to participate at a meaningful, less active level.

Board members have rights, responsibilities and obligations including:

- Books and Records: A member may reasonably require to inspect them or have an accountant or attorney do so.
- Management Access: Directors should feel free to contact the Executive Director (within the bounds of reason) yet restrain themselves from contacting other members of management...members should be careful not to undercut the Executive Director's role or interfere with it.

- Proper Notice: All Directors should be given ample notice of meetings.
- Action: A Director may not ignore what he or she believes to be illegal activity.
- Disclosures: All Directors should complete Financial, Conflict of Interest and Conflict of Commitment forms. Board members who face potential conflict in specific agency activities should disclose this conflict before the Board takes action and provide a disinterested review (not voting or discussing the issue as a matter of record).
- Confidentiality: A Director should not disclose information about the agency's activities unless they are of public record.
- Good Sense: Each member shares in all responsibilities and powers of the Directors. Independent judgment should be exercised by every member of the Board.
- Information: Usually the Board must rely on information provided by staff. This means that the staff must select much of the materials that the Directors receive. Members have a right (and an obligation) to not hesitate to request further, reasonable information if needed.
- Flexibility: Directors should not be satisfied with things-as-they-have-always-been.
- Terms of Office: Each Director should adhere to agency By-Laws regarding length of commitment; remembering that reasonable turnover is extremely healthy for an organization. Many agencies have adopted three years on, one year off terms for the Boards, ensuring that only one third of the Board leaves each year. This has proven to be a very successful policy for most, as during the "year off," many members remain active on committees, etc. and return (if all agree) with new energy.

WHO CARES?

Whoa..what a question. Hopefully, each Board Member cares a great deal about the clients! Additionally, there are others to whom agencies are accountable, namely the states' Attorneys General. Thanks to an endless number of statutes and constitutional provisions, in most of the United States the Attorney General has the authority to hold a Director of a public benefit or religious corporation accountable.

The main role of the Attorney General's office is to ensure that funds are used properly and that the organization is operating for its original charitable purposes. Board Chairs are encouraged to contact their own state's Attorney General's office to obtain a copy of regulations as laws in each state differ slightly.

Although nonprofit organizations have an "obligation" to ensure that donor funds

© 1997, Scribner & Associates

are used appropriately (especially restricted donations), it truly is the Board's role to determine how unrestricted agency funds are to be spent, not the donors'.

All Boards should re-examine their missions and responsibilities from time to time to ensure that they are flexible to changing community and economic issues. Remember, the mission of the organization is to do what is best for the clients, **not** what will ensure the preservation of the nonprofit agency itself!

DON'T LET THE DOOR HIT YOU ON THE WAY OUT
(How to master the art of volunteer "downsizing")

Brrrr. How can you "fire" a volunteer? How rude - after all, they are DONATING their time (as well as their troubles) to the agency.

Phooey.

First of all, drop that assumption. You may think it's easier to "live with" a difficult or invisible volunteer, but rest assured that most of the rest of the Board is not thrilled about it. It often is a terrible drain on the agency.

1. Put your clients in the front of your mind. What is best for them... a well run, involved Board membership. Empty seats do not help at all. Inactivity cannot be acceptable.

2. Drop the word "fire" from your thoughts. The issue is that you want this person to get off the Board seat, not necessarily "go away." In some cases, "going away" is necessary, but usually it's a matter of finding a new (and somewhat distant) role for the person.

3. Accept the fact that YOU MUST DO SOMETHING. It is a matter of "what," not "if."

4. Identify your options. Difficult Board members can be:
   • asked to totally separate from the agency (i.e. testimonial dinner)
   • invited to join endowment councils or special groups
   • invited to become Advisory Council members
   • encouraged to participate in a special project

Is there some issue of special interest to this person? Do you want him or her to maintain a relationship with the organization? If so, be sure it is for the right reason(s). Do not fear "retaliation;" often the person is disliked by everyone else in the community as well. If you are afraid that you may lose promised funds, forget it. Usually, difficult people try to bribe agencies with "potential" gifts that never appear. Even if you know the gift is legitimate, who needs it from that source. Better to put your energies into other, better methods.

5. IF you have a signed Board Contract (or a job description) life will be much easier. Members can be approached based on their difficulty to follow through with their initial commitments... and wouldn't it be better for THEM to find a more appropriate role in the agency. In other words, "we love you still, but OVER THERE."

6. Obviously, the easiest difficult members to "remove" are those who never show up at all. Check your By-Laws. Most organizations have a "three strikes you're out" clause. Write a letter and be done with it. Actually, it really is for their own good as they are as responsible as the rest of the Board even if they don't show up. In some cases you may wish to invite them to join an Advisory Council or something else.

7. Don't bother moving your Board meetings. Difficult people always find them.

8. Bite the Bullet. If the member is active (which many difficult ones are), you must gather your courage, bring another Board member with you and DO IT. You are doing no one any favors by prolonging the inevitable. As a matter of fact, you probably are losing good Board members due to on-going difficulties which can be avoided.

Try a nice approach first...appreciating their efforts and realizing that the position is more than they had probably understood to be the case; that they would be a great help on the Advisory Council or whatever.

Firm approach is next. Clearly both sides aren't happy and it seems that *their* needs aren't being met either.

Regardless of your approach, as in fundraising, you must be SPECIFIC. You must say the words "we believe it is in everyone's best interest, including yours, if you resign from the Board of Directors." SAY IT!

If the situation is extreme (and there are plenty of them), you may have to go back to your By-Laws and vote them off the Board. Be sure to contact legal counsel before making such a move. It must be orchestrated perfectly and legally. Trust me!

Easy? Of course not. Necessary? Absolutely. And it's YOUR job as the Chair to treat your volunteers (and staff, donors, etc.) with the same concern and compasion that you hold for the people you serve. Sometimes that means taking difficult measures. It might mean that some Board members will be angry with you. Some might even resign. *It might also mean that your agency can get on with its real job...*

© 1997, Scribner & Associates

SMILE WHEN YOU SAY THAT!
Board Chairs and Executive Directors

Board Chairs AND Executive Directors...notice the 'AND', not 'VERSUS'! What a terrific partnership these two positions can forge; and what a devastating mess can occur when they work at odds with each other. Not a pretty sight.

As has been mentioned throughout this guidebook, Board members and Chairs have not attended Volunteer University. Well, guess what? There are no Universities for Executive Directors either! Though business degrees and the like are readily available (even MBAs in Nonprofit Managment), nothing can prepare a person adequately to face anywhere from 3 to over a hundred bosses and the world of volunteer/staff management!

Each organization having both a Board Chair and an Executive Director will operate uniquely, depending on the styles and personalities of those individuals. Ideally, Chairs and Executive Directors work in an atmosphere of friendship, support, tolerance and honesty; helping each other with the difficult tasks they face separately and together. Ideally.

Some pairs of leaders have, shall we say, less than ideal relationships. Board Chairs have been equally guilty of undermining Executive Director decisions as Directors have been of working around the Chair to get to the rest of the Board.

Working together as staff and volunteer leaders is similar to getting married for many. In marriage one notices nasty little habits such as missing toothpaste caps and chronic channel surfing. Many of these new discoveries are overlooked or accepted as part of the "whole" of the partnership. The same can be true for volunteer and staff leaders. At first, a few new "quirks" are noticed, i.e. lack of returning phone calls, missing deadlines, etc. In time, however, just as in some marriages, these little annoyances can explode into major, divisive problems; creating barriers and "camps" of support; focusing the energy of the organization on itself and the behavior of its leaders rather than the clients. What a terrible waste of time, talent and energy.

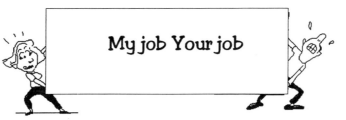

Nonprofit organizations are uniquely faced with staff/volunteer leadership sharing, though many for-profit agencies often have their own Boards with which to deal. Nonprofits, however, often stand an easier chance of resolving problems because they are (or should be) vision driven rather than resource driven. This can make for a bit more willingness to resolve problems. Hopefully.

62

© 1997, Scribner & Associates

Knowing that the relationship between the Chair and the Executive Director has a vital impact on the work of the organization and all staff and volunteers, there is a simple suggestion to strengthen it:

Take a **TIME OUT**. Share information, establish rules and procedures that are comfortable for both leaders. A mini-assumption party would not be a bad start. Having done so personally, a thrown pie can work wonders to break tension (and teeth, so be careful).

Either party can call a "meeting of the minds" to decide how this partnership is going to work. Both individuals, however, must share the desire to work together. If one is not interested, then a positive relationship cannot develop. In this unfortunate situation, Boards are encouraged to bring in outside expertise to help handle the difficulties which can include anything from discussions to actually removing one (or both) of the parties from the situation.

Hoping to avoid such extreme measures, most Executive Directors and Board Chairs can develop agreements between themselves which clarify roles and expectations. Once completed, appropriate decisions should be shared with the Board and staff who, no doubt, are as confused as everyone else.

STEPS TO CREATE A WORKING PARTNERSHIP:

1. Meet at a neutral, private site. Restaurants are not bad. Most agencies are too busy. Find a quiet place where you can talk. Bring paper.
2. Each party should come equipped with his/her job description, a personal WIIFM list and a list of professional goals for the coming year.
3. The Chair should bring a small garbage bag and tiny pieces of paper. A private Assumption Party should be held with each person reading his/her written statements and discussing them with the other. Assumptions which are valid should be kept. Those that are "brain sludge" should be tossed away.

63

© 1997, Scribner & Associates

4. The Chair and the Executive Director should share their WIIFMs with each other - what they hope to personally gain from the experience of working with the agency for the next year or so. This often leads to discussions filled with surprises such as "I didn't know you like snowboarding, so do I!"
5. Each should describe the relationship he or she believes would be ideal between the two positions. Discuss common elements.
6. Together, they should list all the major tasks facing the agency during the next year. Each task should be written on a separate piece of paper. Under the task, columns should be written:

Board   **Staff**   **Committee**   **Chair**   **Executive Director**

The role of each of the above positions (and others as appropriate such as 'donors,' 'clients,' 'advisors,' should be dicussed for *each* task. Take your time, this important discussion may take a while (and may need to be repeated with the Board and staff). Refer to job descriptions, rumors and preferences throughout!

7. Clarify communication (obviously the biggest problem):
    What does the Chair REALLY want/need to know?
    What does the Executive Director REALLY want/need to know?
    How should the Executive Director best reach the Chair?
    What constitutes an emergency? Who should be contacted in such cases?
    How does the Chair expect the Director to interact with the Board? How does the Director expect to do so?
    How does the Director expect the Chair to interact with the staff? How does the Chair feel about this?
    What problems do both want to avoid? How can this happen?
8. Based on tasks, WIIFMs and understandings, the Chair and the Executive Director should create a calendar for the year which includes all appropriate agency meeting dates, special meetings for themselves, trainings, etc.
9. If all else fails, consider a third party from the Board or an outside friend/professional to aid in this discussion. Sometimes the hardest thing is to admit is that you are having difficulties in the first place...keep in mind that your agency and clients are counting on you to work this out.
10. Split the lunch check evenly. Now THERE'S a partnership!

© 1997, Scribner & Associates

WHAT TO INCLUDE IN A CHAIR KIT!

Chairs of Boards are not without resources - unless they want to be! There are a number of people, materials and activities which can help any Chair be most effective and learn how to incorporate the position into their lives (not the other way around!).

1. Aspirin.
2. A sense of humor; permission to have fun.
3. A real gavel. Plastic knives banged on cups do not command attention.
4. Perspective. Get away once in a while.
5. Consistent communication - individual and group.
6. Limits and boundaries (so you can have a life).
7. Clear understanding of your role with others in the agency.
8. Opportunity to attend trainings and leadership development workshops.
9. Willingness to change and grow.
10. On-going connection with agency clients to keep them foremost in your mind.
11. Permission to yourself to make mistakes. Big ones.
12. Permission to forgive yourself.
13. Permission not to know everything.
14. Willingness to let others help and make mistakes. Big ones.
15. Ability to miss a meeting once in a while for the heck of it (nothing rattles up a Board better than that)
16. Access to skills you need - whether in finance, funding, marketing, or program. Surround yourself with others who know more and let them help! People LOVE giving advice.
17. Enough wisdom to listen to others' suggestions. There is a lot to learn.
18. Enough kindness to ensure that everyone is appropriately included in activities ranging from planning to fundraising...build ownership. Remember, process often is more important than product.
19. Respect for all volunteers, staff and members of your agency's "family."
20. Respect for yourself. Know when to stay. Know when to leave.
21. Above all, respect for your clients and what is best for them.

© 1997, Scribner & Associates

Of special note:

People tend to be reluctant to accept the role of Chair because the position appears (and often is) overwhelming. The greatest gift you can provide your agency is to make the position reasonable as well as meaningful. Delegate with kindness and leadership. Help others to learn more. Seek and use advice of others – there is no greater compliment.

Whether you were "rail roaded" into the position or agreed to do so with a happy heart, I hope that this guidebook is of some help to you. And on behalf of clients, volunteers, donors and staff, thank you for all that you do and all that lies ahead.

Sincerely,
Susan M. Scribner

SCRIBNER & ASSOCIATES

Fundraising and Organizational Development
Services, Trainings and Programs

ABOUT SUSAN M. SCRIBNER

Susan Scribner provides on-site assessments, consultation, retreats and training in all aspects of nonprofit financial and organizational development including: **Effective Fundraising Planning, Implementation of Annual and Capital Fundraising Programs, Financial Development Audits, Board Development, Long Range/Strategic Planning, Public Relations Strategies, Endowment Programs, and Volunteer Development.**

All services are designed to help agencies develop practical, usable skills in fundraising and organizational management. Her clients included health care providers, senior centers, organizations serving people with disabilities, social service agencies, organizations for the arts, women's shelters, schools and colleges, and community development projects among others.

For more than twenty five years, Susan has developed customized annual, capital and planned giving programs, and has provided implementation assistance for hundreds of individual agencies and boards. She is the author of *How to Ask for Money Without Fainting*, and *Boards from Hell*, a guide to help strengthen non-profit boards of directors. Her most recent publication, *Are You Chairing a Board by the Seat of Your Pants* is for board and committee leaders and those who love them!

Prior to starting her firm in 1984, Susan conducted a wide variety of annual, capital, endowment and special funding activities. She is the former Executive Director of VIVA in Washington, D.C., a national concern group for POWs and MIAs in Southeast Asia, the organization which created the POW/MIA bracelets. Susan has served as the Director of Development for such organizations as the Greater Southeast Community Hospital Foundation and the seven YWCAs of the National Capital Area in Washington, D.C., as well as other nonprofit agencies. She worked in marketing for the Marriott Corporation and in public and media relations for various organizations. Susan is a former Senior Trainer with the Grantsmanship Center in Los Angeles where she conducted fundraising and board development workshops throughout the country.

Susan currently works closely with Nevsky Angel in St. Petersburg, Russia where her books have been translated and are being distributed throughout the country. She provides on-site organizational development and fundraising consultation to hundreds of newly formed non-government social service groups throughout Russia each year.

As a member of the faculty of the University of Judiasm, Susan taught Advanced Financial Policy and Community Development for the University's MBA program in Nonprofit Management. She also teaches a variety of courses in philanthropy and agency management at other universities. She frequently is called upon to conduct trainings and keynote conferences for such organizations as the National Society of Fundraising Executives, the Josephson Institute for the Advancement of Ethics, UCLA, the Los Angeles Women's Foundation, the Southern California Association of Philanthropy, state departments of Rehabilitation throughout the country and various city Planned Giving Councils. Susan is a Lead Instructor for the Center for Nonprofit Management, and a Consultant/Trainer for Volunteer and Support Centers throughout the U.S., among others. Susan was selected to serve on a Presidential Task Force to create Model Public/Private Partnerships.

Susan has been a member of such organizations as the National Association for Hospital Development, the President's Commission on the Employment of the Handicapped, the National Association of the Deaf and Southern California's Local Management Assistance Providers Council. She is a volunteer Sign Language interpreter, a licensed pilot and winner of the 1969 Transatlantic Air Race from New York to London.

---

49 Coronado Avenue, Long Beach, California 90803
Voice/TDD: (310) 433-6082   Fax: (310) 439-3025   Internet: scribner@aol.com

THE NONPROFIT IN YOUR FACE TRILOGY!

Are You CHAIRING A BOARD by the Seat of Your Pants?

by
Susan M. Scribner

From Electric Chairs to Folding Chairs... there is no Chair College and gavels do not come with instructions!

Identify your (unique?) management styles and steps you may wish to take to make life and leadership easier:

- Finally create job descriptions for leaders
- Really understand By-laws
- Delegation without threats
- Bob's Rules of Disorder (non-deadly meetings)
- And more, more, more!

HOW TO ASK FOR MONEY WITHOUT FAINTING!

by
Susan M. Scribner

Is your financial development raising anything but blood pressure? Raising money works if YOU ASK!

HOW TO ASK FOR MONEY WITHOUT FAINTING includes a great number of tips regarding:

- Clearly articulating your agency's needs
- Determining your best prospects
- Terror free prospect research
- Effective asking techniques
- Oh, so much more!

BOARDS FROM HELL

by
Susan M. Scribner

Phantom Boards, Bored Boards, Boardettes, Boardellos, Mutant Ninja Board Members and more!

Learn what you must do to create a Heavenly Board! This 60 page guidebook includes:

- Identifying Board problems
- Effective roles of Board, staff and committees
- Volunteer recruitment and management
- No More Tears Strategic Planning
- A whole lot more!

ELECTRONIC BOOK COMPUTER DISKS!

Information included in the electronic book versions can be personalized and printed to meet your organizational and fundraising needs! Interactive and easy!

To preview or order ELECTRONIC BOOK VERSIONS:

CAPITOL PUBLICATIONS
1101 King St. Suite 444
Alexandria, Virginia 22314
Call (800) 655-5597   Fax (800) 392-7886

_____ copies of CHAIRING A BOARD @ $15 each $ _____

_____ copies of HOW TO ASK FOR MONEY
         WITHOUT FAINTING @ $12 each $ _____

_____ copies of BOARDS FROM HELL @ $15 each $ _____

[PLEASE RUSH ME]

Shipping: _____ I'm frantic, Rush First Class @ $3.50 per book ($10 max)
          _____ No rush, Fourth Class $1.75 per book   Shipping Total: $ _____
          (appropriate taxes included - discounts available for multiple copies)
                                                    Total: $ _____

_____ Check or _____ Credit Card (circle one): VISA MasterCard American Express Discover

Card No.: _____   Expiration date: _____

Name on card: _____   Phone: _____

Make checks payable to SCRIBNER & ASSOCIATES and mail to:
49 Coronado Ave. Long Beach, CA 90803   (562) 433-6082

Name: _____   Agency: _____

Address: _____ City _____ State _____ Zip _____